S0-ADR-230

Hands-On Serverless Deep Learning with TensorFlow and AWS Lambda

Training serverless deep learning models using the AWS infrastructure

Rustem Feyzkhanov

BIRMINGHAM - MUMBAI

Hands-On Serverless Deep Learning with TensorFlow and AWS Lambda

Copyright © 2019 Packt Publishing

All rights reserved. No part of this book may be reproduced, stored in a retrieval system, or transmitted in any form or by any means, without the prior written permission of the publisher, except in the case of brief quotations embedded in critical articles or reviews.

Every effort has been made in the preparation of this book to ensure the accuracy of the information presented. However, the information contained in this book is sold without warranty, either express or implied. Neither the author, nor Packt Publishing or its dealers and distributors, will be held liable for any damages caused or alleged to have been caused directly or indirectly by this book.

Packt Publishing has endeavored to provide trademark information about all of the companies and products mentioned in this book by the appropriate use of capitals. However, Packt Publishing cannot guarantee the accuracy of this information.

Commissioning Editor: Amey Varangaonkar
Acquisition Editor: Nelson Morris
Content Development Editor: Ronnel Mathew
Technical Editor: Dinesh Pawar
Copy Editor: Safis Editing
Project Coordinator: Hardik Bhinde
Proofreader: Safis Editing
Indexer: Rekha Nair
Graphics: Tom Scaria
Production Coordinator: Jyoti Chauhan

First published: January 2019

Production reference: 1310119

Published by Packt Publishing Ltd.
Livery Place
35 Livery Street
Birmingham
B3 2PB, UK.

ISBN 978-1-83855-160-5

www.packtpub.com

`mapt.io`

Mapt is an online digital library that gives you full access to over 5,000 books and videos, as well as industry leading tools to help you plan your personal development and advance your career. For more information, please visit our website.

Why subscribe?

- Spend less time learning and more time coding with practical eBooks and Videos from over 4,000 industry professionals

- Improve your learning with Skill Plans built especially for you

- Get a free eBook or video every month

- Mapt is fully searchable

- Copy and paste, print, and bookmark content

Packt.com

Did you know that Packt offers eBook versions of every book published, with PDF and ePub files available? You can upgrade to the eBook version at `www.packt.com` and as a print book customer, you are entitled to a discount on the eBook copy. Get in touch with us at `customercare@packtpub.com` for more details.

At `www.packt.com`, you can also read a collection of free technical articles, sign up for a range of free newsletters, and receive exclusive discounts and offers on Packt books and eBooks.

Contributors

About the author

Rustem Feyzkhanov is a machine learning engineer at Instrumental. He works on creating analytical models for the manufacturing industry. He is also passionate about serverless infrastructures and AI deployment. He has ported several packages on AWS Lambda, ranging from TensorFlow/Keras/sklearn for machine learning to PhantomJS/Selenium/WRK for web scraping. One of these apps was featured on the AWS serverless repository's home page.

Packt is searching for authors like you

If you're interested in becoming an author for Packt, please visit `authors.packtpub.com` and apply today. We have worked with thousands of developers and tech professionals, just like you, to help them share their insight with the global tech community. You can make a general application, apply for a specific hot topic that we are recruiting an author for, or submit your own idea.

Table of Contents

Preface

This book prepares you to use your own custom-trained models with AWS Lambda to achieve a simplified serverless computing approach without spending much time and money. By the end of the book, you will be able to implement a project that demonstrates the use of AWS Lambda in serving TensorFlow models.

Furthermore, we will cover deep learning and the TensorFlow framework. We will look at how to train neural networks, but more importantly, we will cover how to use pretrained neural networks in your application and where you can find them. After that, we will look into how to deploy deep learning applications using the serverless approach. We will also cover their advantages, disadvantages, possible limitations, and good practices.

Later on, we will build a number of applications that will utilize the serverless deep learning approach. We will make a planning API and take a look at the AWS API Gateway service, and explore how to deploy everything in a convenient way. In the later stages, we will make a deep learning pipeline and an AWS simple query service. We will explore how to use it with AWS Lambda and showcase how to deploy the application.

Who this book is for

This course will benefit data scientists who want to learn how to deploy models easily, and beginners who want to learn about deploying into the cloud. No prior knowledge of TensorFlow or AWS is required.

What this book covers

Chapter 1, *Beginning with Serverless Computing and AWS Lambda*, goes through all the examples that we are planning to look at. We will also describe the serverless concept and how it has changed the current cloud infrastructure environment. Finally, we will see how serverless deep learning allows us to make projects that are much easier to implement than traditional deployment techniques, while being just as scalable and cheap.

Chapter 2, *Starting Deployment with AWS Lambda Functions*, introduces AWS Lambda and explains how to create an AWS account. We will make our first Lambda and see how to easily deploy it using the Serverless Framework.

Chapter 3, *Deploying TensorFlow Models*, introduces the TensorFlow framework, along with several examples on how to train and export a model. Also, we will look at the repositories of pretrained models that anyone can use for their own tasks. Finally, we will show how to import pretrained models that is required for your projects.

Chapter 4, *Working with TensorFlow on AWS Lambda*, digs into the specifics of how to start working with serverless TensorFlow. Also, we will see small details of how serverless TensorFlow is different from traditional deployment from the perspective of cost, scale, and speed. We will also look at how to start with using the standard AWS UI, and then understand how the same can be done using the Serverless Framework.

Chapter 5, *Creating the Deep Learning API*, explains how to make a deep learning REST API. Then we will introduce AWS API Gateway and learn how to make the application using two methods: AWS UI and the Serverless Framework.

Chapter 6, *Creating a Deep Learning Pipeline*, explains how to make a deep learning pipeline application. We will introducte AWS SQS and explain how to make the application using two methods: AWS UI and the Serverless Framework.

Chapter 7, *Creating a Deep Learning Workflow*, explains how to make a complex deep learning algorithm application. We will introduce AWS Step Functions and explain how to make the application using two methods: AWS UI and the Serverless Framework.

To get the most out of this book

Basic knowledge of AWS Lambda and Python is required to get the most out of this book.

Download the example code files

You can download the example code files for this book from your account at www.packt.com. If you purchased this book elsewhere, you can visit www.packt.com/support and register to have the files emailed directly to you.

You can download the code files by following these steps:

1. Log in or register at www.packt.com.
2. Select the **SUPPORT** tab.
3. Click on **Code Downloads & Errata**.
4. Enter the name of the book in the **Search** box and follow the onscreen instructions.

Once the file is downloaded, please make sure that you unzip or extract the folder using the latest version of:

- WinRAR/7-Zip for Windows
- Zipeg/iZip/UnRarX for Mac
- 7-Zip/PeaZip for Linux

The code bundle for the book is also hosted on GitHub at `https://github.com/PacktPublishing/Hands-On-Serverless-Deep-Learning-with-TensorFlow-and-AWS-Lambda`. In case there's an update to the code, it will be updated on the existing GitHub repository.

We also have other code bundles from our rich catalog of books and videos available at `https://github.com/PacktPublishing/`. Check them out!

Download the color images

We also provide a PDF file that has color images of the screenshots/diagrams used in this book. You can download it here: `http://www.packtpub.com/sites/default/files/downloads/9781838551605_ColorImages.pdf`.

Conventions used

There are a number of text conventions used throughout this book.

`CodeInText`: Indicates code words in text, database table names, folder names, filenames, file extensions, pathnames, dummy URLs, user input, and Twitter handles. Here is an example: "In the `serverless.yml` version, there is name of the function, available resources, and region."

A block of code is set as follows:

```
model.fit(x_train, y_train, epochs=2)
print('Evaluation:')
print(model.evaluate(x_test, y_test))
```

Any command-line input or output is written as follows:

```
npm install -g Serverless
serverless --version
```

Bold: Indicates a new term, an important word, or words that you see onscreen. For example, words in menus or dialog boxes appear in the text like this. Here is an example: "Next, go to the **Users** page and click on **Add user**."

Warnings or important notes appear like this.

 Tips and tricks appear like this.

Get in touch

Feedback from our readers is always welcome.

General feedback: If you have questions about any aspect of this book, mention the book title in the subject of your message and email us at customercare@packtpub.com.

Errata: Although we have taken every care to ensure the accuracy of our content, mistakes do happen. If you have found a mistake in this book, we would be grateful if you would report this to us. Please visit www.packt.com/submit-errata, selecting your book, clicking on the Errata Submission Form link, and entering the details.

Piracy: If you come across any illegal copies of our works in any form on the Internet, we would be grateful if you would provide us with the location address or website name. Please contact us at copyright@packt.com with a link to the material.

If you are interested in becoming an author: If there is a topic that you have expertise in and you are interested in either writing or contributing to a book, please visit authors.packtpub.com.

Reviews

Please leave a review. Once you have read and used this book, why not leave a review on the site that you purchased it from? Potential readers can then see and use your unbiased opinion to make purchase decisions, we at Packt can understand what you think about our products, and our authors can see your feedback on their book. Thank you!

For more information about Packt, please visit packt.com.

Beginning with Serverless Computing and AWS Lambda

1

This book will encourage you to use your own custom-trained models with AWS Lambda and work with a simplified serverless computing approach. Later on, you will implement sample projects that signify the use of AWS Lambda for serving TensorFlow models.

In this chapter, we will discuss serverless deep learning and you will explore why serverless is so popular and the advantages of deploying applications using serverless. Also, you will look into the data science process and how serverless can enable an easy and convenient way to deploy deep learning applications. You will also briefly look into the sample projects that we will make in the forthcoming chapters.

You will also get to learn about the workings of the AWS implementation, including the traditional and serverless ways of deploying deep learning applications.

In particular, we will cover the following topics:

- What is serverless computing?
- Why serverless deep learning?
- AWS Lambda function
- Sample projects

What is serverless computing?

Serverless computing is a type of architecture for which the code execution is managed by a cloud provider, which means that the developers do not have to worry about managing, provisioning and maintaining servers when deploying the code.

Let's discuss the possible ways of application deployment:

- **On-premise** deployment, let's you control the entire infrastructure including the hardware. In other words, it means that the application runs on our machine, which you can access physically.
- Then, you have **Infrastructure as a Service (IaaS)**, which means that you can't access the servers physically, but you control everything that is happening in it.
- Next, you have **Platform as a Service (PaaS)**, where you don't control the operating system or runtime, but you can control our code and container.
- Finally, you have **Function as a Service (FaaS)** which is a serverless model, and the only thing which you control is the code itself. It can significantly enable us to work on different applications.

Why serverless deep learning?

Let's understand why the severless infrastructure is extremely useful for deploying deep learning models in a data science process.

The usual data science process looks like:

- Business understanding: You need to understand the business needs, which includes defining the objectives and the possible data sources.
- Data acquisition: You need to look into the data you are planning to use, explore it, and try to find correlations and gaps.
- Modeling: You start with the selection of most promising features, building the model, and training it.
- Deployment: You need to operationalize the model and deploy it.
- Customer acceptance: You can provide the result to the customer and receive feedback.

The preceding points are represented in the following diagram:

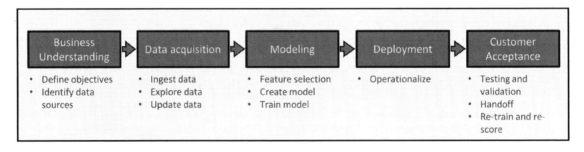

Based on the feedback received from the customer, you can update the model and change the way you deploy it. The deployment and customer acceptance phases are iterative in nature. It means that you will have to get feedback from the user as early as possible. To achieve this, our infrastructure for the deployment has to be both simple and scalable at the same time, which can be done with the help of serverless infrastructure used for deploying the deep learning models.

 You need to be aware that our deep learning infrastructure has to be integratable with our existing infrastructure.

Where serverless deep learning works and where it doesn't work?

Serverless deep learning deployment is very scalable, simple, and cheap to start. The downsides of it are the time limitations, CPU limitations, and memory limitations.

Where serverless deep learning works?

In the following section, you will start by reiterating the advantages of serverless deep learning deployment:

- It is extremely useful for your project. If you train your model and want to show it to the world, serverless deep learning will allow you to do so without complicated deployment and any upfront costs. AWS also provides free usage per month. It means that a number of invocations in AWS Lambda will be completely free. For example, in the image recognition project, which we will discuss in the following chapters, the number of runs will be about 100,000 times.

- Serverless deep learning is great for early-stage startups that want to test their business hypotheses as early as possible. Simplicity and scalability allows small teams to start without expertise in AWS. AWS Lambda allows you to calculate the cost per customer in an easy way and to understand your startup cost per user.

- Serverless deep learning is extremely convenient if you already have an existing infrastructure and want to optimize your costs. Serverless architecture will be a lot simpler and cheaper than the cluster one and it will be easier to maintain. Significantly, it reduces costs since you don't need to retain the unused servers.

- Serverless deep learning would be extremely useful for cases where you have extremely high loads. For example, a lot of companies struggle to maintain the system in cases where there are 1 million requests during the first minute and zero requests in the next minute. The cluster will either be too large or it will take a certain time to scale. Serverless, on the other hand, has unmatched scalability, which allows the system to work on high load without rolling.

Where serverless deep learning doesn't work?

Deep learning will not work in the following situations:

- If one of the main features of your system is to provide a real-time response that is a very complex model; for example, if it is the part of an interaction between your user and the system, then the serverless architecture may not be enough for you. AWS Lambda has a cold start delay and the delay for the unloading and loading of the model into the memory. It does work fast, but it may take more than several seconds to run. Speed highly depends on the size and complexity of the model, so this is something you have to test beforehand.
- Serverless deep learning may fail if your model utilizes a lot of data. AWS Lambda has certain limitations, such as three gigabytes for run and half a gigabyte for the hard disk, which means you either have to optimize your code in terms of memory usage or use the cluster.
- If your model has requirements on the CPU power or number of cores, then it may not be able to start on Lambda. There are no certain limits that could predict whether your model will or will not be able to start on AWS Lambda, so it is something which you need to test.
- An extremely complex model may not work well on serverless infrastructure. By complex, we mean larger than 1 or 2 gigabytes. It would take more time to download it from S3, and Lambda may not have enough memory to load it.

These use cases mentioned above have shown us the landscape for the uses of serverless learning and it will help us to make a decision as to whether to use it or not. Finally, in a lot of cases, there isn't a definitive answer and it makes sense to continue testing your model on serverless.

Now we'll discuss the Lambda function as a serverless model.

Lambda function – AWS implementation of FaaS

In this section, we will discuss the workings of the AWS implementation of FaaS. The Lambda function is an AWS implementation of FaaS. The AWS service keeps Lambda configuration, which is basically code, libraries, and parameters within the service. Once it receives the trigger, it takes the container from the pool and puts the configuration inside the container. Then, it runs the code inside the container with the data from the event trigger. Once the container produces results, the service returns it in the Response.

The following diagram is a representation of the workings of the Lambda function:

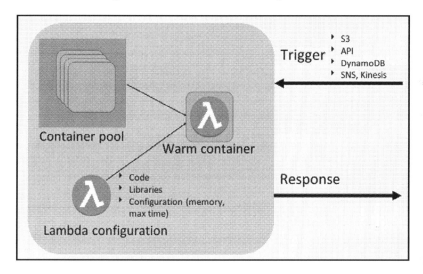

Lambda scales automatically for up to 10,000 concurrent executions. Also, Lambda pricing is a pay per use service, so you would only have to pay for each round of Lambda that you use and you don't have to pay when it doesn't run.

The Lambda configuration consists of the following:

- **Code**: This is what you want to run within the function. The code needs to have an explicit declaration of the function, which you want for the service to run.
- **Libraries**: These enable us to run more complicated processes. You will need to keep them inside the same package as the code itself.
- **Configurations**: These are various parameters that dictate how Lambda works.

The main parameters are as follows:

- The relational memory and time out
- The runtime (for example, Python or node)
- Triggers, which we will describe in the next section
- IAM role, which provides Lambda access to other interval services
- Environmental parameters, which allow us to customize the input parameter to our code

Lambda triggers

There are various AWS services that can act as a trigger for AWS Lambda, they are:

- **DynamoDB**: This enables us to start the Lambda function on each new entry to the database
- **Amazon S3**: This helps the Lambda function start files in the bucket
- **CloudWatch**: This enables us to run Lambda functions according to the shadow (for example, each minute, each day, or only at noon each Thursday)
- **Lex**: This starts by looking at what the usual data science process looks like
- **Kinesis, SQS, and SNS**: These enable us to start the Lambda function on each object in the event stream

There are a lot of different triggers, which means you can bind Lambda with a lot of different services.

Why deep learning on AWS Lambda?

Here, you will see the advantages of AWS Lambda :

- Coding on an AWS Lambda is very easy. You will just need the package code and libraries, not the Docker containers. It enables you to start early and deploy the same code, which you would run locally. This is therefore perfect for early stage projects.
- AWS Lambda is extremely scalable and, more importantly, you don't have to manage the scalability or write separate logic for it because your data science application will be able to easily process a large number of tasks or work with multiple users.

- AWS Lambda is priced conveniently. You only need to pay for what you're actually using and the price itself is very affordable. For example, for the image recognition model, the cost will be $1 for 20,000 to 30,000 runs.

In the next section you will know the difference between traditional and serverless architecture using Lamda.

Traditional versus Serverless architecture using Lambda

Let's look at the difference between traditional and serverless architecture. The following diagram represents the deep learning API through traditional architecture:

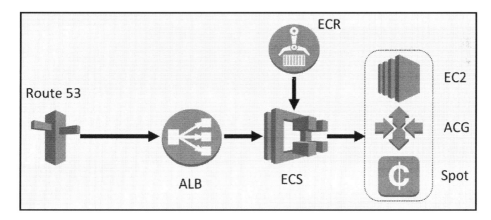

In the above traditional architecture, you will not only have to handle the cluster itself, but you will also have to handle all the balancing of API requests. Also, you have to manage the Docker container with the code and libraries and find a way to deploy it using the container registry.

You need to have extensive knowledge of AWS to understand this architecture. Although it is not very difficult, it can be a real issue to begin with. You will need to keep in mind that the AWS architecture for deep learning will have static costs.

Let's discuss the serverless implementations of the above application. The following diagram represents the architecture for deep learning using Lambda:

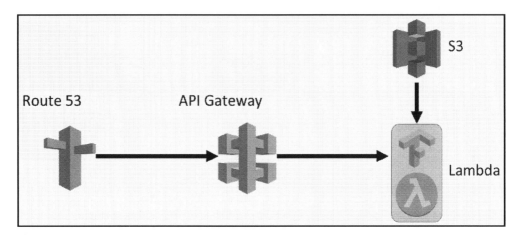

In the preceding diagram, you can see that it looks a lot easier than traditional architecture. you don't need to manage node balance scalability or containers—you just need to put in your coated libraries and Lambda manages everything else. Also, you can make a number of different prototypes with it and you will only need to pay for invocations. This makes Lambda the perfect way for making your deep learning model available to users. In the next section, you briefly be introduced to the projects that you will develop in this book.

Sample projects

In this section, you will cover projects, which you will develop during the course of this book. you will create three projects:

- Deep learning API
- Deep learning batch processing
- Serverless deep learning workflow

Deep learning API

The deep learning API project provides a great hands-on experience since you are able to see results immediately from your browser. You will start with the deep learning API for image recognition. Image recognition is one of the tasks where deep learning shows incredible results, which are impossible to implement using any other approach. you will be using a contemporary, publicly available pre-trained inception model, which is version free. This project will also show you how easy it is to take an open source model and create an API interface on it.

Deep learning batch processing

In the deep learning batch processing project, you will take a closer look at how a lot of companies run deep learning applications nowadays. In this project, you will build deep learning batch processing for image recognition. It will show us how high Lambda scalability allows us to process thousands of prediction drops at the same time.

Serverless deep learning workflow

In the serverless deep learning workflow project, you will highlight the patterns of deep learning models on the serverless infrastructure. You will make a serverless deep learning workflow for image recognition. This project will show you how you can use contemporary deployment techniques using AWS step functions. You will also learn how you can conduct A/B testing of the model during deployment, error handling, and a multistep process. This project will help you to understand the possible applications of serverless deployment and how to apply this knowledge to either your personal project or within your company.

Summary

In this chapter, you were introduced to the serverless functions, the AWS implementation, and the services. You looked at the Lambda function, which is an AWS implementation of FaaS. You also covered the workings of the AWS implementation of FaaS. Later, you understood why the serverless infrastructure is extremely useful for deploying deep learning models and the challenges you might face during its deployment. You also compared the traditional and serverless ways of deploying deep learning applications. You looked into the possible scenarios where the serverless deep learning works and where it doesn't work. Finally, you covered the various example projects that you will be learning about during the course of this book.

In the next chapter, you will learn how to work with AWS Lambda and its deployment.

Starting Deployment with AWS Lambda Functions 2

In this chapter, we will understand more about AWS Lambda and learn how it works. We will also discuss the different ways of deploying Lambda and the things we need to consider while developing applications for AWS Lambda.

We will learn how to set up an AWS account along with access management. We will also create a Hello World function using AWS Lambda.

We will cover the following topics:

- AWS Lambda functions
- Getting started with AWS account
- Introduction to Serverless framework
- Deploying AWS Lambda functions

Technical Requirements

The technical requirements in this chapter are as follows:

- AWS subscription
- Python 3.6
- AWS CLI
- Serverless framework
- You can find all the codes at `https://github.com/PacktPublishing/Hands-On-Serverless-Deep-Learning-with-TensorFlow-and-AWS-Lambda`

AWS Lambda functions

Let's go through the pre-requisites of AWS Lambda as shown here:

```
import sys, os
import mylib
...
def handler(event, context):
  ...
  print("Hello world log")
  return result
```

It consists of the following steps:

1. Importing libraries, which you have already installed on AWS Lambda. This includes system libraries and a number of AWS-specific libraries. You don't have to include these libraries within your package.

2. Importing external libraries, from other developers and companies, or your own libraries. You need to include them in your package.

3. Implementing `handler` function which handles processing of the requests to the main variables as input event and context. The `event` is trigger-specific information and `context` is information about Lambda, which handles requests. It contains the ID and parameters of the function.

4. Process the request.

5. Return the `result`, this will either be provided back to the trigger in the event of a synchronous execution or it'll be saved to the log in the event of asynchronous execution.

 You need to keep in mind that you can't use any context or state other than the one which comes from the trigger. Also, if you print something during the code's execution, it will be saved to the local stream of the function.

Pros, cons, and limitations of AWS Lambda

There are certain pros, cons, and limitations of AWS Lambda, as described here:

- **Pros**: AWS Lambda is very easy to deploy. We don't have to know the Docker or other container frameworks to manage it. It should only contain libraries and code. AWS Lambda easily connects to triggers, which means that we can easily integrate it with various other infrastructures and it is very scalable as well, which makes it extremely useful for production deployment. It is relatively inexpensive too.
- **Cons**: It may be difficult hard to debug in the various Lambdas locally. You have to recreate the entire environment and libraries and also be able to check your memory consumption during timeout. Making good estimations of how fast you will be able to produce high peak loads is quite difficult with AWS Lambda. AWS Lambda is stateless and it greatly effects how you organize your application. This means that the stage should come from the trigger.
- **Limitations**: There are certain limitations with RAM, disk, CPU, and timeout which you have to consider during development.

The following diagram describes the pros, cons, and limitations in detail:

Pros	Cons	Limits
<ul><li>Easy to deploy (no Docker)</li><li>Easy to connect to triggers (API, S3, SQS, DynamoDB)</li><li>Easy to scale</li><li>Relatively cheap</li></ul>	<ul><li>No local debug</li><li>Unpredictable warm containers</li><li>Stateless</li></ul>	<ul><li>Max 3 GB RAM</li><li>Max 500 MB disk</li><li>Max 5 min execution time</li><li>CPU is proportional to provisioned memory</li></ul>

Now that we have a fair idea with the pros, cons, and limitations of AWS Lambda, let us have a look at the basics of creating an AWS account.

Getting started with AWS account

In this section, you will learn about the AWS free tier and the IAM. We need to have an AWS account to learn in depth.

 If you do not have an AWS account, you can sign up here: `https://aws.amazon.com/account/`.

The Lambda API Gateway, the simple queue service, and functions are a part of the AWS Free Tier, so you won't be charged for a small amount of consumption.

AWS Free Tier

The Free Tier allows you to have free usage of AWS services. It covers a number of different AWS services like:

- **AWS Lambda**: This covers 1 million invocations, which makes a Lambda perfect for hosting your pet project
- **AWS API Gateway**: This covers 1 million requests through a paid gateway, so it can be extended to work on the project with an AWS REST API functionality
- **AWS SQS**: This includes 1 million simple queue services and requests
- **AWS step functions**: This includes 4,000 state transitions of step functions, which will allow us to create free serverless workflows

Identity and Access Management (IAM)

There are two types of accesses that you can create for an AWS user:

- **AWS management control access**: This allows you to use AWS web services. The user needs to have a login ID and password, which the user will use online.
- **Programmatic access**: This allows you to use an AWS software development key. The user needs two keys: the access key ID and a secret access key.

Now, let's a create a user with programmatic access. It will allow us to use a serverless framework, which will manage the deployment and orchestration of AWS Lambdas.

In order to create the user, we will follow the below steps:

1. First, you need to go to the AWS dashboard and choose the IAM service, as shown in the following screenshot:

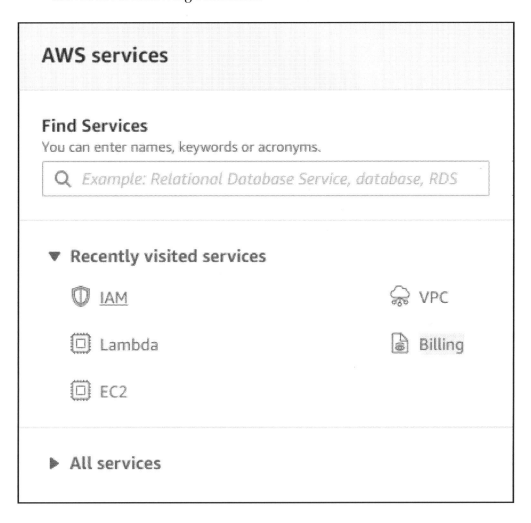

2. Next, go to the **Users** page and click on **Add user**, as shown here:

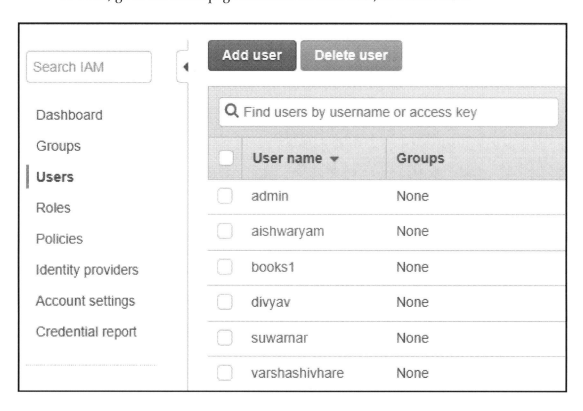

3. Now, set up the name, `lambda`, and select the **Programmatic access** checkbox:

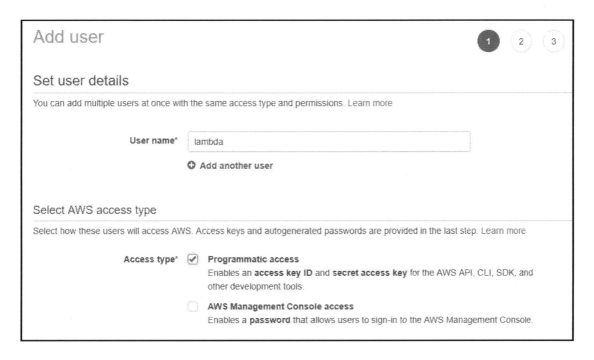

4. Next, you will need to set permissions for the user to use the AWS services discussed earlier. The easiest way to do that is by choosing **Attach existing policies directly** and then choosing the **AdministratorAccess** policy, as shown in the following screenshot:

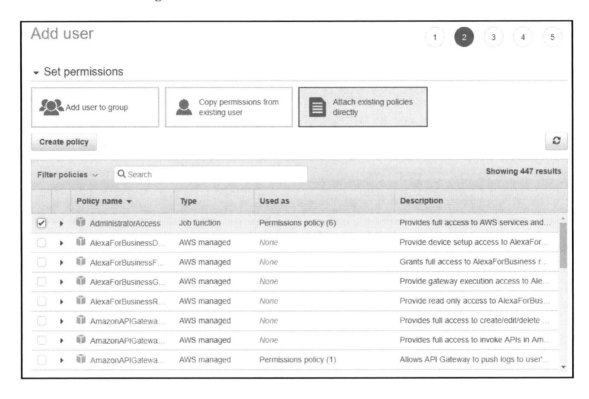

5. Finally, you need to confirm all the choices:

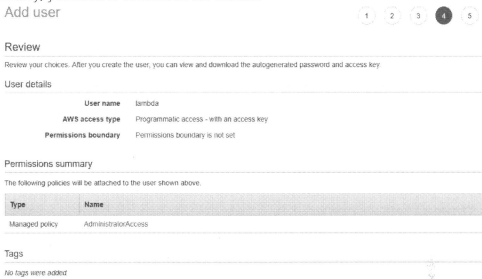

6. It will show us the access key ID and secret access key. You can either copy them from the web service or save them through the CSV file. You will need these access keys later while setting up the serverless framework, as shown here:

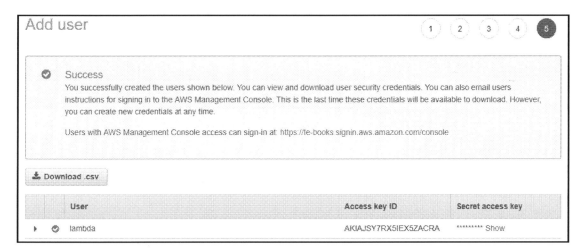

In the next section, we will create a hello word AWS Lambda function.

Creating a Hello World AWS Lambda function

There are three primary ways to create a Hello World an AWS Lambda from the AWS console:

- We can create a Lambda from scratch. It is the easiest way to create a simple Lambda.
- We can use existing blueprint to create a Lambda. AWS has a catalog of usages for any base Lambda, and you can use it to start with a Lambda, which is closer to the project you want to create.
- In 2018, AWS added serverless application repositories where users can submit their Lambda configurations. The repository has hundreds of different Lambda packages and it is extremely useful to create a Hello World in AWS Lambda.

Using the Lambda function

We'll discuss the ways of using the Lambda function with the following points:

- You can use the inline editor in AWS Service Cloud 9. It can be very helpful in cases where you don't want to install anything locally and want to keep all your files in the cloud. The drawback is that it can be pretty challenging to automate deployment with the inline editor, as well as handling complex side libraries and large projects with multiple files.
- You can upload a ZIP file with libraries and code, either through the web interface or through the command line. This is a very straightforward process, which you can easily automate. The main drawback of this approach is that the package has a 50 MB limitation on size.
- The best and the most popular way to upload the package is through the S3 bucket. It doesn't have a 50 MB limitation for the package, although, a 250 MB limit for our ZIP libraries and the code will still be in place.

AWS Lambda code

Perform the following steps to create the Hello World code:

1. Log in with your `lambda` IAM user. Go to the AWS console and choose the AWS Lambda service:

2. Click on **Create a function,** as shown in the following screenshot:

3. Choose **Author from scratch,** as shown here:

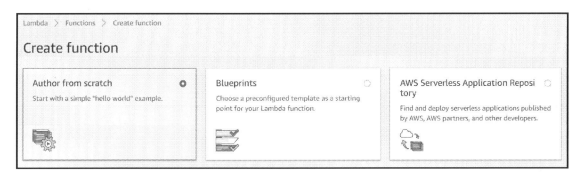

4. We need to add a **Name**, **Runtime**, and **Role**. Then , we need to add a **Role name**, helloLambda. For **Policy templates**, select **Simple microservice permissions** and click on the **Create function** button, as shown in the following screenshot:

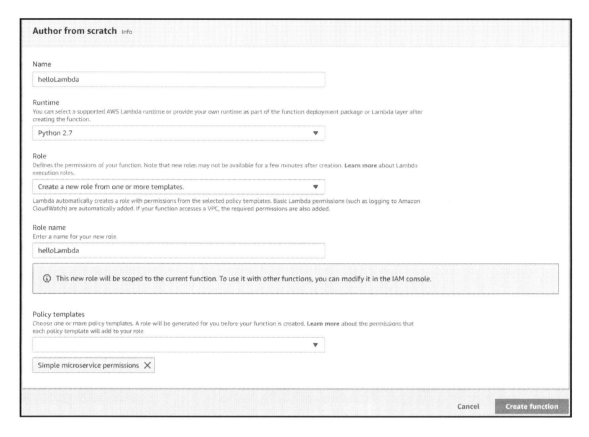

5. Finally, we get the interface of AWS Lambda. We get the connected triggers, code editor, and settings:

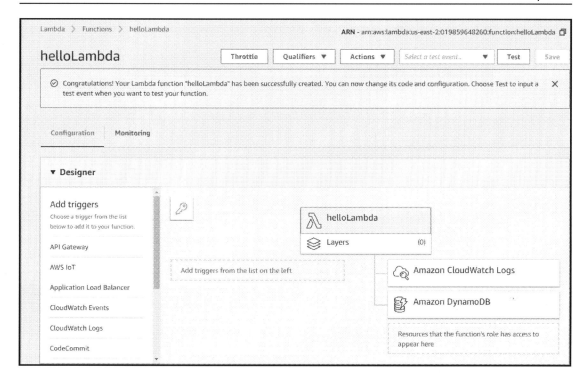

6. You need to configure the test event and start your first Lambda function. For our first Lambda function, you can just make an empty event:

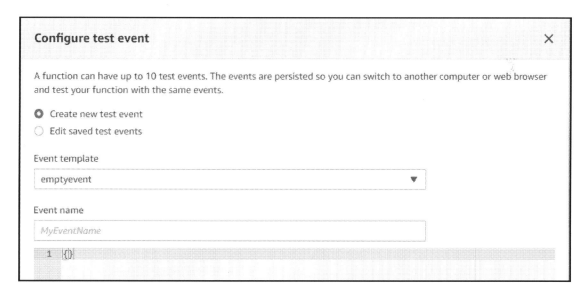

7. Edit the code and save it and you'll see that a Lambda has been updated:

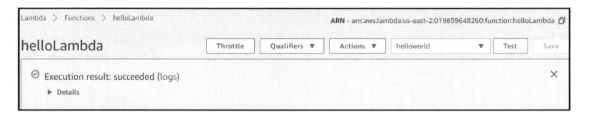

In the next section, we will learn about the serverless framework.

Introduction to the serverless framework

In the previous sections, we learned about the different ways to deploy the Lambda function. Although the Lambda package is just ZIP files with libraries and codes, there are ways to deploy them as mentioned below. A production usage deployment needs to have the following features:

- First of all, the serverless framework should have a single configuration file where we can set all the options and parameters of deployment. This will allow us to save time while writing long scripts for starting each service separately and it will enable us to keep versions of our environment.
- It should be able to create and attach other AWS services to add to a Lambda. Since most use cases involve a Lambda working as a part of a bigger infrastructure, deploying other parts of infrastructure separately can be a huge issue.
- Having a convenient command-line interface helps a lot because not only would it mean that you can deploy everything using a single script but also set up automatic deployment.

Features of the serverless framework

A serverless framework has a number of useful features. They are as follows:

- It is open source, which means that the serverless community helps to build and maintain the framework. This allows the framework to be free and up-to-date.

- The serverless framework supports different public cloud platforms, such as AWS Google call functions and Azure functions. It means that you don't have to learn how the UI works for either of the mentioned services. You can use the same common UI to deploy functions on another service.
- The serverless framework has a production-level quality and a number of companies use it for deploying the serverless infrastructure.
- It has a plug-in system, which allows users to create custom plugins for the frameworks. It allows serverless to have various functionality; for example, supporting step functions.

Installation of the serverless framework

In order to install the serverless framework, we need to install the following functions:

- We will need to install Node and NPM (`https://nodejs.org/download/`). The serverless framework is written in JavaScript, so it requires Node for execution and NPM for handling the packages.
- We will need Python (`https://www.python.org/downloads`) and `pip` (`https://pip.pypa.io/en/stable/installing/`) to run Lambda code locally and we will need it in the various command-line interfaces.
- We will need the AWS command-line interface (`https://docs.aws.amazon.com/cli/latest/userguide/installing.html`), for the serverless framework to connect to your AWS account. Then, we can install the serverless framework and everything will be configured.

 The complete installation process of the serverless framework can be found here `https://serverless.com/framework/docs/providers/aws/guide/installation`.

Installing the serverless framework is extremely easy. We just need to run the following command:

```
npm install -g serverless
```

We can check that it works by running the following command:

```
serverless --version
```

This will return the version of the installed serverless framework.

Deploying AWS Lambda functions using the serverless framework

We will start with what the serverless deployment process looks like:

- We have code and libraries for a Lambda execution. These are the same libraries and code that you would see if you uploaded your package directly as a ZIP. In that sense, it is very easy to start deploying existing Lambdas through the serverless framework.
- We have a configuration file, which basically contains all the information about how a Lambda will be deployed.

Configuration file

The Lambda configuration file consists of the same parameters, which we have discussed in an earlier section (for example, name, runtime, memory, and timeout). There are three primary differences.

You are not only setting up triggers but also setting up services, in which the triggers depend on. You can set up specific roles and access. Some accesses will be automatically set, but some will need to be configured by you. Finally, you can set up additional plugins, which you will use during deployment. We will look at them in more detail when we deploy the step functions.

Deployment process

This section covers the process of deployment, which will be generated in the custom cloud formation file based on our configuration file. Cloud formation is an AWS service, which allows us to automatically deploy multiple services. This is extremely convenient for handling the deployment process, but its notation can be pretty difficult to start with. That is why we are using the server's configuration file, which is more readable. Next, the service framework packages libraries and code in a single package and uploads which will then run the AWS cloud formation service for deployment by using the file generated previously.

Now, let's move on to the actual deployment of a Lambda, using the serverless framework, by looking at the available files.

There are two files: `index.py` and `serverless.yml`. Let's look at `index.py`. The following code will print the input event and return the `Hello World` message, as shown in the following snippet:

```
def handler(event,context):
    print('Log event',event)
    return 'Hello world'
```

The following snippet shows the `serverless.yml` file:

```
service: helloworld

frameworkVersion: ">=1.2.0 <2.0.0"

provider:
  name: aws
  region: us-east-1
  runtime: python3.6
  memorySize: 128
  timeout: 10

functions:
  main:
    handler: index.handler
```

In the `serverless.yml` version, there is the name of the function, the available resources, and the region. `helloworld` is the name of the service, which we deploy. `main` is the name of the function and `index.handler` is the name of the `index.py` file and the name of the function inside of their file handler.

One service may have different functions and that is why they are separated. Before deploying them, we can run a Lambda locally. This is one of the good features of the serverless framework, but it may not work with complex libraries because of the differences in OS. We can see that we printed an empty log and received the `Hello World` message as output:

```
C:\Users\test\Desktop\V12024_Codes\Serverless-Deep-Learning-with-TensorFlow-and-AWS-Lambda-master\lesson2.6>serverless i
nvoke local --function main
('Log event', {})
"Hello world"
```

Before deploying Lambda, you need to link your AWS account to serverless using following command:
```
serverless config credentials --provider aws --key "Your
access key" --secret "Your secret access key"
```

You will deploy a Lambda using the serverless framework. Also, even if you have a simple program, it may take some time for the serverless framework to deploy the service:

```
C:\Users\test\Desktop\V12024_Codes\Serverless-Deep-Learning-with-TensorFlow-and-AWS-Lambda-master\lesson2.6>serverless deploy
Serverless: Packaging service...
Serverless: Excluding development dependencies...
Serverless: Creating Stack...
Serverless: Checking Stack create progress...
.....
Serverless: Stack create finished...
Serverless: Uploading CloudFormation file to S3...
Serverless: Uploading artifacts...
Serverless: Uploading service .zip file to S3 (492 B)...
Serverless: Validating template...
Serverless: Updating Stack...
Serverless: Checking Stack update progress...
..............
Serverless: Stack update finished...
Service Information
service: helloworld
stage: dev
region: us-east-1
stack: helloworld-dev
api keys:
  None
endpoints:
  None
functions:
  main: helloworld-dev-main
layers:
  None
```

Now, you can run the Lambda code and check the output:

```
C:\Users\test\Desktop\V12024_Codes\Serverless-Deep-Learning-with-TensorFlow-and-AWS-Lambda-master\lesson2.6>serverless invoke local --function main
('Log event', {})
"Hello world"
```

As you can see, it is the same as the one we received earlier. There are two great flags, which really helps when working with a Lambda. The first flag helps to send custom events inside a Lambda, thereby, emulating triggers from the custom service and the log allows you to see the log of the current execution. This flag log will allow us to look at the log, and the data flag will allow us to send a custom message.

Summary

In this chapter, we learned about AWS Lambda functions, along with getting started with AWS account. We also learned about creating a Hello World AWS Lambda function, along with an introduction to the serverless framework and deployment of AWS Lambda functions.

In the next chapter, we will start deploying TensorFlow models, where we will learn more about TensorFlow models and how to deploy them.

Deploying TensorFlow Models 3

In this chapter, we will discuss the TensorFlow framework. Initially. We will begin by describing how the various approaches for building the algorithms differ. We will also cover deep learning and how to train neural networks but, more importantly, you will learn how to use pre-trained neural networks in the application and where you can find them.

We will cover the following topics:

- Approaches for building algorithms
- Why neural networks?
- Repositories for pre-trained TensorFlow models
- An example of image captioning

Technical Requirements

- AWS subscription
- Python 3.6
- AWS CLI
- Serverless framework
- You can find all the codes at `https://github.com/PacktPublishing/Hands-On-Serverless-Deep-Learning-with-TensorFlow-and-AWS-Lambda`

Approaches for building algorithms

The various approaches for building algorithms are :

- First of all, there are deterministic algorithms that are very transparent and predictable, but it may be very difficult to build a custom algorithm for complex tasks, which will work in all cases.

- Next, there's the machine learning technique, where we train the model based on features we get from data. We don't need a lot of data to train models in a reliable way, but we need to make a separate process for training validation and testing.
- Finally, there's the deep learning approach, where we train our own neural networks. The main advantage of this is that we can use raw data without predefined features. The downside is that we need a lot of data and a lot of computing resources for training.

The machine learning approach varies greatly from the classic approach. The classic approach uses rules and data as input and answers as output. In the machine learning approach, we use data and answers as input and we produce rules as output, as shown here:

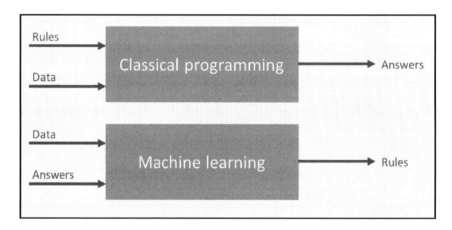

Let's look into why neural networks have become so popular in recent years.

Why neural networks?

The reasons why neural networks have become popular in recent years are as follows:

- Computing resources have become a lot cheaper now compared to the prices in the past. With the introduction of a public cloud, it became extremely easy and affordable to use these resources at scale.
- The machine learning approach requires a lot of data and, right now, there's a lot of public and private data that can be used for training.
- Advanced algorithms were allowed to make and train more complex neural networks.

Let's discuss why we actually don't need to train neural networks to successfully use them.

Pre-trained networks

Although training neural networks may require large processing power and a lot of data, deploying them can be done using a simple CPU. In this way, we can say that deploying a deep learning model is close to using an external library in your code. Secondly, there's a large community of people and companies that open source their pre-trained neural networks, which means that you can freely use them.

There are two instances where using pre-trained neural networks can be extremely convenient:

- The first case is when your task has already been solved. For example, if you want to conduct image captioning with *X* classification, then you can use already existing neural networks.
- The second case is when your task is fairly different from what has been done but it's close. Then, you can use pre-trained models to generate features that you can use later with deterministic or simple machine learning models.

Majority of the pre-trained models use TensorFlow and therefore it currently is the most popular framework for deep learning. It has a very large community of people and a lot of people share the models they've trained. Most companies that are using neural networks in their production environment are using the TensorFlow framework. We will, therefore, learn the use of TensorFlow for the pre-trained models through an example in the next section.

Simple TensorFlow example

One of the great use cases for showing the power of deep learning is the **MNIST** (short for **Modified National Institute of Standards and Technology**) dataset. It consists of black and white pictures with handwritten digits, as shown in the following image:

Each image is labeled based on the digit that's written on the image. The task, in this case, is to predict the label based on the image. This kind of task is very difficult to implement using deterministic methods; as you can see in the preceding image, there are a lot of different ways of writing the same number. Therefore, you can't use a single template for prediction.

Training for MNIST

In this section, we'll discuss model training for MNIST:

1. First, we start with importing the `tensorflow` library. For this example, we'll use the Keras deep learning framework, which makes it easy to set up layers for the neural network. In simple terms, Keras acts as a wrapper on top of TensorFlow, so everything is still based on TensorFlow.

2. Next, we need to load data and present it in a binary format since the original image pixel values are 0 and 255. We'll also divide the dataset into training and test sets. This will allow us to measure the performance of the neural network. A good practice for the machine learning approach is to train the model on the training dataset and measure the final score on the test dataset. It enables us to be sure that the model doesn't see data points on which it'll be measured after training. We'll see the explanation as follows:

   ```
   import tensorflow as tf

   mnist = tf.keras.datasets.mnist

   (x_train, y_train),(x_test, y_test) = mnist.load_data()
   x_train, x_test = x_train / 255.0, x_test / 255.0
   ```

3. Now, we need to set up the layers for our neural network. Basically, each layer consists of a number of neurons and an activation function. In this case, the first layer tries to get more useful data out of the raw data. The second layer tries to use this data to assign the probability of the image being one of 10 digits.

4. As part of the model, you need to choose three parameters for the training process:
   - First is the `loss` function, which the network will use to optimize its performance. The training process basically consists of decreasing the value of the `loss` function and trying to find weights for the neural network, so the `loss` function will be minimal.

- Next is the `optimizer`, which handles how the neural network will iterate towards the most optimal solution, and how it'll change weights after each iteration.
- Finally, `metrics` allows us to measure neural network performance over the dataset. For example, `accuracy` allows us to understand which part of the dataset was correctly classified. This metric doesn't participate in the training process directly and mainly allows us to understand whether network performance has improved or not. We can understand the preceding explanation from the following code:

```
model = tf.keras.models.Sequential([
  tf.keras.layers.Flatten(),
  tf.keras.layers.Dense(512, activation=tf.nn.relu),
  tf.keras.layers.Dense(10, activation=tf.nn.softmax)
])
model.compile(optimizer='adam',
              loss='sparse_categorical_crossentropy',
              metrics=['accuracy'])
```

5. Once everything is set up, we can just run training on the training part of our dataset. It may take several minutes, depending on the configurations of your computer. After that, we can evaluate model performance and the test set. Our model will produce something around 97% accuracy/test set, which is very impressive, and as demonstrated, it can be achieved with even a simple neural network as shown in the code below:

```
model.fit(x_train, y_train, epochs=2)
print('Evaluation:')
print(model.evaluate(x_test, y_test))
```

6. Finally, once the neural network has been trained, we can save it so that we can use it later. As you can see, it's a pretty simple process. The model file will contain the model architecture, a key composition of layers, the layer's weights and training configuration, and the optimizer state, which allows us to continue training on the already trained model:

```
model.save('MNISTmodel.h5')
modelImported = tf.keras.models.load_model('MNISTmodel.h5')
print('Evaluation by imported model:')
print(modelImported.evaluate(x_test, y_test))
```

Let's discuss the available files. There's only one Python file, the `testMNIST.py` file, which we're about to run. In this file, we can see the parts that we've discussed, which include data transformation, model installation, model training, model evaluation, model export, and model import.

Now, let's run the `testMNIST.py` file in the command line to see the results. By running the code, we can see the process of training, which happens in epochs. This kind of neural network doesn't require a GPU to train and we can achieve very good results, even on the CPU:

```
python testMNIST.py
```

As you can see in the following screenshot, we achieved 97% accuracy with just two epochs and were able to successfully export and import the model. We can see the exported retrained model, which can now be used in different code:

```
60000/60000 [==============================] - 18s 295us/step - loss: 0.0822 - a
cc: 0.9750
Evaluation:
10000/10000 [==============================] - 0s 42us/step
[0.078011581791564482, 0.9753]
```

.In the next section, we talk about the repositories for pre-trained TensorFlow models.

Repositories for pre-trained TensorFlow models

The pre-trained models are pretty skilled when it comes to import and export. In a nutshell, declaring deployment consists of importing the trained model and transforming input data into the format that's acceptable by the neural network. There are certain things that you need to keep in mind during deployment:

- The model can be pretty large, for example, hundreds of megabytes, which makes deployment more difficult.
- We need to keep versions of the model and track their performance. If you train the model by yourself, you might need to update the model based on changes in incoming data or if you find better architecture.
- Some models require additional files that translate predicted numbers or values into meaningful information.

TensorFlow repository

TensorFlow has five main repositories with a number of selected models. They're a bit established and it's very easy to use them with the TensorFlow framework.

 For more information on the most popular models that are trained using TensorFlow, visit this site: `https://github.com/tensorflow/models`.

The different examples for the repositories are as follows:

- Image to text models, which allow what's happening on the image to be described
- Image captioning, which classifies the image
- Deep speech, which allows speech to be recognized
- Text summarization, which allows you to make a summary of the text article
- Vid2depth, which produces a depth map based on the video stream

TensorFlow Hub

There's the TensorFlow Hub hosting platform, which was specifically designed for neural networks. TensorFlow Hub has a lot of great models that are free to use and are mainly trained by Google. They're good and are of state-of-the-art quality. The advantage of TensorFlow Hub is that the models are checked before they're added and the disadvantage is that it has a high barrier for entry submissions.

 TensorFlow Hub for different models can be viewed at the following link: `https://tfhub.dev/`.

GitHub

GitHub is considered the largest repository of open source code. There are countless models that are published there but, since there's no entry filter, you'll need to be more cautious about using these models in production. The advantage of GitHub is that it has a low barrier for entry and the disadvantages are that it may be difficult to find a relevant model and the user needs to check how the model works before deployment.

In this next section, we learn about Image captioning through an example.

Image captioning example

Image captioning is a task where we need to recognize an object on the image. Although it sounds simple, it was considered one of the most difficult problems in computer vision since it was close to impossible to make a separate detector for each type of object. The main way to test the image captioning algorithm is to run it on the ImageNet dataset. The ImageNet dataset consists of 14 million images with over 20,000 labels. It was introduced in 2010. Every year, there's a competition of different models, and accuracy has significantly improved in recent years due to the introduction of complex neural networks.

There are a number of different models with different architectures that successfully work with ImageNet. We'll see that errors significantly decreased over the years. The following diagram shows a change in the error rate of winner models in the ImageNet dataset.

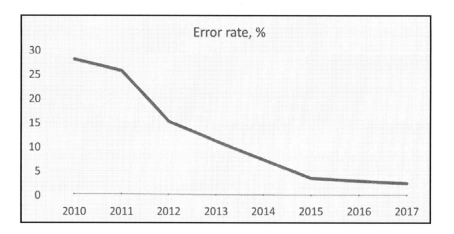

We'll now discuss Inception v3, which we'll use in the code sample later.

Inception v3

Inception v3 was introduced by Google and achieved an error rate of 3.46%. You'll see that Inception v3 is significantly more complex. It also takes more resources to train this model, but the upside here is that we don't have to train it to use it.

We'll look into what we'll need to start using Inception v3 in our code. The model consists of layers and weight values present in `classify_image_graph_def.pb`.

We also have a list of labels, which the model can predict in `imagenet_2012_challenge_label_map_proto.pbtxt` file and a document that allows the mapping of results of the neural network to the labels in `imagenet_synset_to_human_label_map.txt` file.

Here's an example of the Panda image. First, we receive the IDs that score. The highest score means that the model has high confidence in the image having this label. After mapping IDs to label names, we can see that the model correctly detected Panda. The following screenshot explains this:

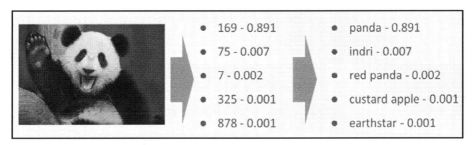

TensorFlow code for Inception v3

Now, let's see how the code for any Inception v3 model will look like:

1. First, we need to set up a TensorFlow session. A session is an environment in which tensors are evaluated.
2. We need to read and set up our neural network by loading it from the file.
3. Next, we need to ask for our image in the format that'll be readable by the neural network.
4. We will need to run a power model and receive a list of row predictions, and transform these predictions into actual label values, as shown in the following code:

```
SESSION = tf.InteractiveSession()
softmax_tensor = tf.get_default_graph().get_tensor_by_name('softmax:0')

predictions = SESSION.run(softmax_tensor,{'DecodeJpeg/contents:0':
image_data})

node_loolup.id_to_string(predictions)
```

Running the code

Let's look at the available files, `inputimage.png` and `testinception.py`, which we're about to run. In this example, we'll be using the Panda image (`inputimage.png`).

1. As shown in the following code, there's the `NodeLookup` class, which will help us to translate responses from the model to the label name:

```
class NodeLookup(object):
    """Converts integer node ID's to human readable labels."""
```

2. The following code shows how we can read the image:

```
image = 'inputimage.png'
image_data = tf.gfile.FastGFile(image, 'rb').read()
```

3. Then, this is the code that tells how we import the pre-trained model:

```
with tf.gfile.FastGFile('classify_image_graph_def.pb', 'rb') as f:
    graph_def = tf.GraphDef()
    graph_def.ParseFromString(f.read())
    tf.import_graph_def(graph_def, name='')
```

4. Here, we exchange the model:

```
SESSION = tf.InteractiveSession()
softmax_tensor =
tf.get_default_graph().get_tensor_by_name('softmax:0')

predictions = SESSION.run(softmax_tensor,{'DecodeJpeg/contents:0':
image_data})
```

5. Finally, we translate the results of the model:

```
predictions = np.squeeze(predictions)
node_lookup =
NodeLookup(label_lookup_path='imagenet_2012_challenge_label_map_pro
to.pbtxt',
  uid_lookup_path='imagenet_synset_to_human_label_map.txt')

top_k = predictions.argsort()[-5:][::-1]
strResult = '%s (score = %.5f)' %
(node_lookup.id_to_string(top_k[0]), predictions[top_k[0]])
print()
for node_id in top_k:
    human_string = node_lookup.id_to_string(node_id)
    score = predictions[node_id]
    print('%s - %s (score = %.5f)' % (node_id, human_string,
```

```
score))
```

6. Now, we can run the code and see the response. As you can see from the following output, the model successfully detected a panda on the image. The code will run fast since there's no training involved. You can try the code on different images and get a sense of the possibilities of this model:

```
(base) D:\lesson3.4>python testInception.py
WARNING:tensorflow:From testInception.py:61: FastGFile.__init__ (from tensorflow
.python.platform.gfile) is deprecated and will be removed in a future version.
Instructions for updating:
Use tf.gfile.GFile.
2019-01-29 20:43:16.474582: W tensorflow/core/framework/op_def_util.cc:355] Op B
atchNormWithGlobalNormalization is deprecated. It will cease to work in GraphDef
 version 9. Use tf.nn.batch_normalization().
2019-01-29 20:43:16.716582: I tensorflow/core/platform/cpu_feature_guard.cc:141]
 Your CPU supports instructions that this TensorFlow binary was not compiled to
use: AVX2

169 - giant panda, panda, panda bear, coon bear, Ailuropoda melanoleuca (score =
 0.89342)
103 - ice bear, polar bear, Ursus Maritimus, Thalarctos maritimus (score = 0.002
77)
7 - lesser panda, red panda, panda, bear cat, cat bear, Ailurus fulgens (score =
 0.00215)
163 - American black bear, black bear, Ursus americanus, Euarctos americanus (sc
ore = 0.00143)
61 - brown bear, bruin, Ursus arctos (score = 0.00122)
```

Summary

In this chapter, we studied different approaches for building algorithms. We discussed how to train TensorFlow models and repositories for pre-trained Tenserflow models. We also learned about image captioning using an Inception v3 TensorFlow example.

In the next chapter, we'll learn how to work with TensorFlow AWS Lambda, where we'll learn more about using TensorFlow models with AWS Lambda.

4
Working with TensorFlow on AWS Lambda

In this chapter, we will learn about the architecture of deploying TensorFlow with AWS, and we will deploy TensorFlow on AWS Lambda using the pre-existing pack and the serverless framework.We will also look into the various general issues with deploying the various Python frameworks on AWS Lambda and then cover all of the solutions to the same issues.

We will cover the following topics:

- Architecture of deploying TensorFlow with AWS Lambda
- General issues with deploying Python frameworks on AWS Lambda
- Deploying TensorFlow on AWS Lambda using pre-existing pack
- Deploying TensorFlow using a serverless framework

Technical Requirements

- AWS subscription
- Python 3.6
- AWS CLI
- Serverless framework
- You can find all the codes at: `https://github.com/PacktPublishing/Hands-On-Serverless-Deep-Learning-with-TensorFlow-and-AWS-Lambda`

Architecture of the deploying TensorFlow with AWS Lambda

In this section, we will learn about the architecture of deploying TensorFlow with AWS Lambda. One of the critical questions of deployment is about where to keep the retrained model that will be used within AWS Lambda.

There are the following three possible options:

- Keep the model within the deployment package alongside the code and libraries
- Keep the model on the S3 bucket and unload it in AWS Lambda during execution
- Keep the model on the FTP or HTTP server and unload it into AWS Lambda during execution

Model within the deployment package

This option means that the model is within the deployment package. The code will import it from a local filesystem. This option has its own pros and cons.

Pros

The advantages of the model within the deployment package are as follows:

- We will get a very good start speed for our deployment since there is no overhead on the loading model
- We will have a single package to start with
- We won't need any outside servers or AWS services as part of our deployment

Cons

The disadvantages of the model within the deployment package are as follows:

- There is considerable limitation on the package size and it limits the possible size of our model
- In the case where you need to manage different versions of the model, it may be tricky to either keep them all in one package or deal with different versions of your package

Model on the S3 bucket

This option means that we have to keep the model in the S3 bucket and unload it during AWS Lambda execution. This option is very limited in terms of package size.

Pros

The advantages of the model on the S3 bucket are as follows:

- At first glance, it will be limited to only 500 MB of usage, which is the maximum size of TMP folder on AWS Lambda, but it is actually possible to download the model directly into memory by passing this limit
- It will be a lot easier to manage multiple models as you can use AWS Lambda environmental variables to procure equipment links to S3 bucket for each of the models that you want to use

Cons

The disadvantages of the model on the S3 bucket are as follows:

- We will get a slower start than in previous cases, since Lambda will need to download the model first
- It should be noted that, though it happens only during cold start, during warm start, the model will already be in memory
- You will need to make the S3 bucket upload all of your models as a part of your deployment, and add logic for managing the different models within the code

Model on the HTTP/FTP server

This option is mostly useful for the case where you want to limit the use of AWS services, memory or integrate with services outside of AWS. The AWS Lambda downloads the model from HTTP or FTP server during deployment.

Pros

The advantages of the model on the HTTP/FTP server are as follows:

- You can use a number of publicly available services with models
- You don't have to update your model on S3 bucket or within the package

Cons

The disadvantages of the model on the HTTP/FTP server are as follows:

- It may be even slower than with the previous case, which is a downside of this model
- Due to the slower time, you will need to make sure that the server is available from your location

General issues with deploying Python frameworks on AWS Lambda

In this section, we will learn about AWS Lambda main limit, which is also known as the size of the package. The current limit for the Lambda deployment package is 50 MB. It is supposed to include libraries and code. There are two main libraries that we need to fit:

- TensorFlow
- NumPy

These libraries are used for matrix calculations. As you may know, the libraries by themselves are pretty big and they just wouldn't work on AWS Lambda. As you have already seen in the previous section on deployment that when we deploy them through S3, we don't have this limitation, and we only have 250 MB limitation for the unzipped package. In this case to make it work, we need to reduce the size of the package.

Solutions for issues with deploying Python frameworks on AWS Lambda

There are a number of ways as to how we can reduce the package size. Here are the solutions for the issues in question:

- We can compress the shared libraries; this usually enables us to get the best reduction of size.
- We can remove the `.pyc` files as they do not influence the library work.
- Next, we can remove tests and visualization folders from the libraries as they are not useful in production.

- Next, we can remove libraries that already exist on AWS Lambda.
- Finally, we can check and remove the libraries that aren't used during execution, for example, wheel or PIP libraries.

Now, in the following code, there is the part that finds and compresses all shared libraries. Then, we find and delete all .pyc files.

The following screenshot shows the commands for the preceding explanation:

```
find -name "*.so" | xargs strip
find -name "*.so.*" | xargs strip

find . -name \*.pyc -delete
```

Next, we need to delete libraries that won't be used during execution, such as .pip and wheel. Finally, we can also delete some folders from TensorFlow library.

The following screenshot shows the different commands for the preceding explanation:

```
rm -r pip*

rm -r wheel*

rm easy_install.py

find . -type d -name "tests" -exec rm -rf {} +
```

The whole process of preparing a package for AWS Lambda can be done through Docker. You don't need to use it for the project we will create, but it is good to keep in mind how to prepare this kind of package.

To install Docker, you just need to run three comments in your comment line:

1. You need to get the latest Amazon Linux image on which we will run the script.
2. You need to start a Docker container with the managing output folder inside the container.

3. You can run the script inside the container and it will assemble the package for you. The following screenshot displays all of the commands to install Docker:

```
docker pull amazonlinux:latest

docker run -v $(pwd):/outputs --name lambdapackgen -d
amazonlinux:latest tail -f /dev/null

docker exec -i -t lambdapackgen /bin/bash
/outputs/buildPack.sh
```

Deploying TensorFlow on AWS Lambda using the pre-existing pack

In this section, we will learn to deploy TensorFlow on AWS Lambda using the pre-existing pack. In the project files, we have model files that are also known as the model itself and files that enable us to translate model response through labels. In Inception folder and Lambda package, which is also known as the code and libraries in lambdapack folder.

To run the code, we need to do the following:

- We'll create S3 bucket where we will keep the model and upload the model itself
- Then,we'll modify code for the specific bucket and add the created bucket name
- Lastly, we can package it and upload to add the AWS Lambda

Now, we will create S3 bucket using the AWS Console and upload files there. We will open the code and add the bucket that we have just created. Then, let's package it and upload it to add AWS Lambda.

We will have to follow the given steps:

1. We need to go to the S3 service and click **Create bucket**:

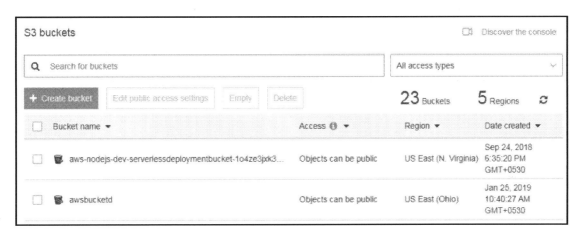

2. Now, we can choose the bucket name:

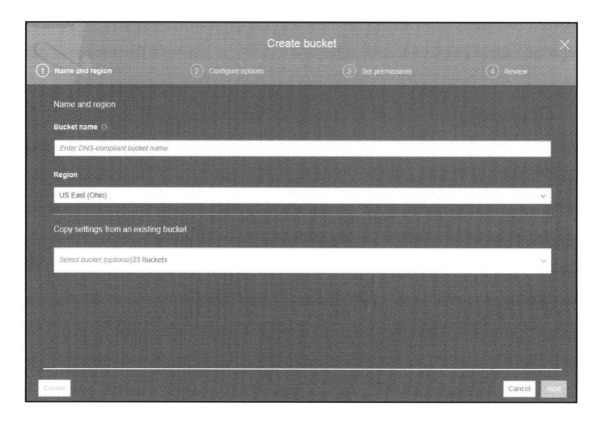

3. Once we have the bucket in place, we can upload files there. You just need to click **Upload** and then choose files. So, here we just upload the package with libraries, and it will start the upload process, along with the package itself. We will need to upload model files, which are present in the `Inception` folder:

4. You can see that now we have a package inside our S3 bucket:

Name ▾	Last modified ▾	Size ▾	Storage class ▾
📁 Imagenet	...	...	...
📁 Lambdapack	...	...	...
📄 serverlessDeepLearning.zip	Jan 30, 2019 1:19:35 PM GMT+0530	52.6 MB	Standard

5. Now, we have to create the role for our AWS Lambda, which we can do from the IAM service:

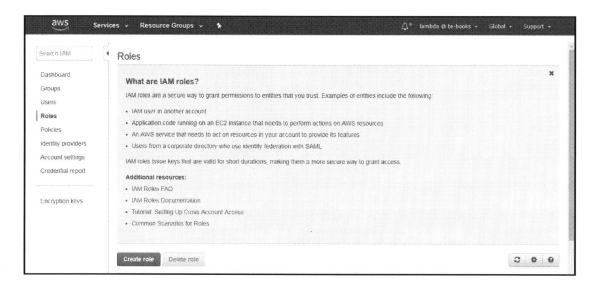

6. We need to choose **Lambda** and click on **Next: Permissions**, which lies at the bottom-right of your screen:

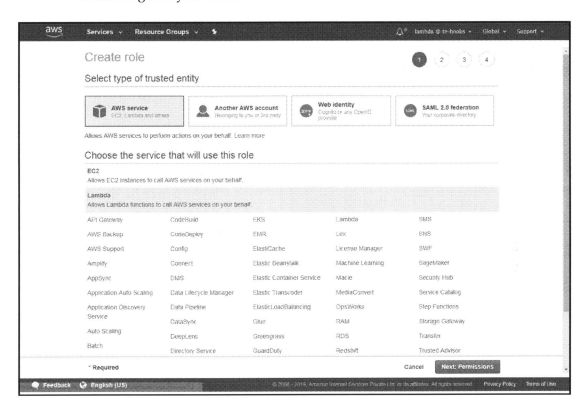

7. For simplicity, it is easier to choose administrator access and click on **Next: Tags,** which lies at the bottom-right of your screen. This would allow our Lambda to access all services. Usually in production, the role is limited to accessing only specific services. We will cover this when we work with serverless frameworks:

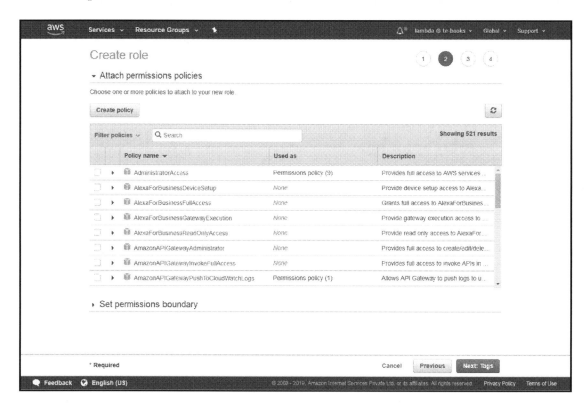

8. Create a role name: `lambdaAdminRole`, which will create the role in Lambda:

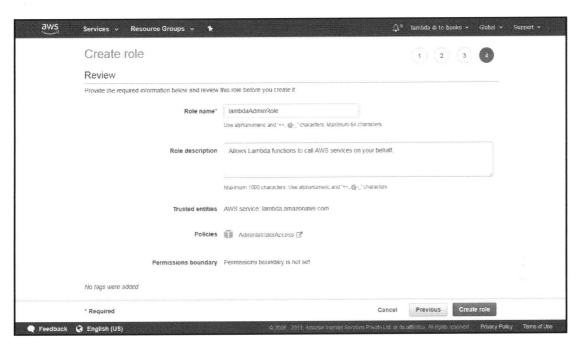

9. To create Lambda, navigate to Lambda function and create the function. Here, enter the name `testensorflolambda`, **Runtime** as **Python 3.6**. For **Roles**, select **Choose an existing role**, and in **Existing role**, select `lambdaAdminRole`, then click on **Create function** at the bottom-right corner:

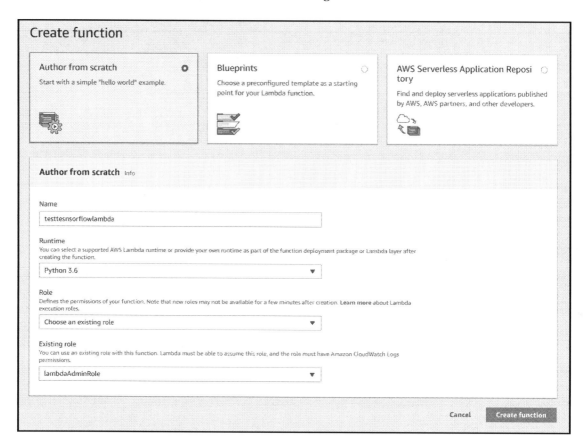

10. After the function is created, we need to change the **Handler** to `index.handler`:

11. On the same screen, scroll down and, in the **Basic setting** tab, add enough resources as presented in the following screenshot:

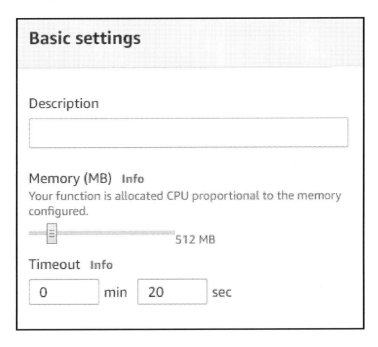

12. Pass the link with the URL of our package (S3 bucekt) and click on **Save** in the top right corner:

13. You can see the function is created. To test the function, click on the **Test** on the top-right corner:

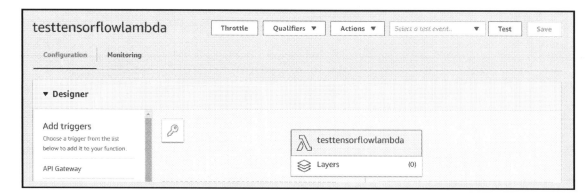

14. After the function is tested, it will successfully produce the following result:

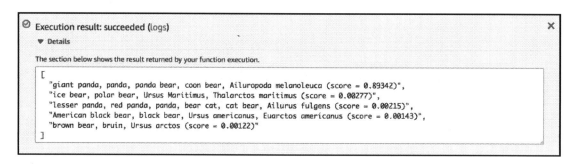

Deploying TensorFlow using a serverless framework

First, we will look at the project files. We have model files in the `Inception` folder, and Lambda code with `Serverless.yml`, the configuration file in the `Lambdapack` folder.

The flow of deployment will be the same as in the previous section. One of the main differences will be that, instead of providing an AWS Lambda admin role, we will provide access to bucket by serverless CML file. The only thing we need to add is `bucketname`, and run the properties of access as shown:

```
...
    iamRoleStatements:
     - Effect: "Allow"
       Action:
         - "s3:*"
       Resource:
       - " arn:aws:s3:::bucketname/* "
...
```

We will need to create an S3 bucket, upload files there, and then deploy AWS Lambda. We will create an S3 bucket and upload files from the command line: `aws s3 sync.s3://<bucket>/.`

Creating a bucket

We will first need to create a bucket, then we will need to upload model files to the bucket, run serverless, and start the AWS Lambda.

Index.py

Let's look at the available files. We will look at the `index.py` file as shown:

```
import boto3
import numpy as np
import tensorflow as tf
import os.path
import re
from urllib.request import urlretrieve
import json
SESSION = None
strBucket = 'serverlessdeeplearning'
def handler(event, context):
 global strBucket
 if not os.path.exists('/tmp/imagenet/'):
 os.makedirs('/tmp/imagenet/')
strFile = '/tmp/imagenet/inputimage.jpg'
```

The main difference is that we run the code inside the `handler` function and we need to download the model files and image file from the S3 bucket:

```
if not os.path.exists('/tmp/imagenet/'):
 os.makedirs('/tmp/imagenet/')
strFile = '/tmp/imagenet/inputimage.jpg'
downloadFromS3(strBucket,'imagenet/inputimage.jpg',strFile)
global SESSION
 if SESSION is None:
downloadFromS3(strBucket,'imagenet/imagenet_2012_challenge_label_map_proto.
pbtxt','/tmp/imagenet/imagenet_2012_challenge_label_map_proto.pbtxt')
downloadFromS3(strBucket,'imagenet/imagenet_synset_to_human_label_map.txt',
'/tmp/imagenet/imagenet_synset_to_human_label_map.txt')
 image = os.path.join('/tmp/imagenet/', 'inputimage.jpg')
 strResult = run_inference_on_image(image)
return strResult
def run_inference_on_image(image):
```

Also, we can use one of the advantages of AWS Lambda. We can save model files as global variables. Basically, we can define session as a global variable. With these, if we start Lambda right after the previous Lambda was executed, all model files will be in the RAM memory:

```
global SESSION
 if SESSION is None:
downloadFromS3(strBucket,'imagenet/imagenet_2012_challenge_label_map_proto.
pbtxt','/tmp/imagenet/imagenet_2012_challenge_label_map_proto.pbtxt')
downloadFromS3(strBucket,'imagenet/imagenet_synset_to_human_label_map.txt',
'/tmp/imagenet/imagenet_synset_to_human_label_map.txt')
 image = os.path.join('/tmp/imagenet/', 'inputimage.jpg')
 strResult = run_inference_on_image(image)
return strResult
def run_inference_on_image(image):
 image_data = tf.gfile.FastGFile(image, 'rb').read()
 global SESSION
 if SESSION is None:
 SESSION = tf.InteractiveSession()
 create_graph()
```

Serverless.yml

In the `Serverless.yml` file, we need to define access to the S3 bucket as that's where we will keep our model. Other than that, it will look exactly as the previously mentioned serverless CML files for other Lambdas:

```
service: deeplearninglambda
frameworkVersion: ">=1.2.0 <2.0.0"
provider:
  name: aws
  region: us-east-1
  runtime: python3.6
  memorySize: 1536
  timeout: 60
iamRoleStatements:
 - Effect: "Allow"
 Action:
 - "s3:ListBucket"
 Resource:
 - arn:aws:s3:::serverlessdeeplearning
 - Effect: "Allow"
 Action:
 - "s3:GetObject"
 Resource:
 - arn:aws:s3:::serverlessdeeplearning/*
functions:
 main:
 handler: index.handler
```

Also, the we need `inputimage.jpg` image for the inception model.

Let's look at the files that we need to upload to S3 bucket:

```
C:\Users\Admin\Desktop\Serverless\Inception>ls
classify_image_graph_def.pb  imagenet_2012_challenge_label_map_proto.pbtxt  imagenet_synset_to_human_label_map.txt  inputimage.png
```

There are two very convenient commands; one allows us to create a bucket, and another allows us to easily upload files into the bucket:

- `aws s3api create-bucket --bucket serverlessdeeplearning`
- `aws s3 sync . s3://serverlessdeeplearning/imagenet`

Since we already have model files in this bucket, there is no need to hold it now, but you can use this command to upload to your bucket. Next, we can return back to the folder with our function and run `serverless deploy` command.

Now, we will invoke the function with the following command:

```
serverless invoke --function main
```

As you can see, it successfully recognized the image. Also, if we invoke the function one more time after that, it will work faster:

```
    "giant panda, panda, panda bear, coon bear, Ailuropoda melanoleu
ca (score = 0.89342)",
    "ice bear, polar bear, Ursus Maritimus, Thalarctos maritimus (sc
ore = 0.00277)",
    "lesser panda, red panda, panda, bear cat, cat bear, Ailurus ful
gens (score = 0.00215)",
    "American black bear, black bear, Ursus americanus, Euarctos ame
ricanus (score = 0.00143)",
    "brown bear, bruin, Ursus arctos (score = 0.00122)"
```

Summary

In this chapter, we learned about the architecture of the deploying TensorFlow with AWS Lambda, in which we covered the possible options of deploying TensorFlow with AWS Lambda along with each of its pros and cons. We also discussed the general issues with deploying Python frameworks in AWS Lambda along with its solutions. Lastly, we deployed TensorFlow on AWS Lambda using the pre-existing pack and using a serverless framework.

In the next chapter, we'll create deep learning API using AWS Lambda.

Creating the Deep Learning API

5

In the previous chapter we learned about working with TensorFlow on AWS Lambda. This chapter briefs about the RESTful API along with the AWS API Gateway. We will learn how to create the API Gateway using the serverless framework.

In this chapter , we will be covering the following topics:

- API service
- The AWS API Gateway
- Creating a deep learning API project

Technical Requirements

The technical requirements in this chapter are as follows:

- AWS subscription
- Python 3.6
- AWS CLI
- Serverless framework
- You can find all the codes at: `https://github.com/PacktPublishing/Hands-On-Serverless-Deep-Learning-with-TensorFlow-and-AWS-Lambda`

RESTful API

The RESTful API has become extremely popular in recent years, with the rising popularity of macro services as a universal way to communicate between different services inside an application—for example, we can use RESTful API services for different programming languages and different hosting platforms together in a single application.

The RESTful API is an interface that allows you to communicate between different applications, and it can serve a lot of purposes. The RESTful API enables you to easily integrate different services. It also allows you to make an easy connection between the frontend and backend of an application, and it allows other developers to use your service. The deep learning API, in this context, allows you to easily integrate deep learning models within your application or provide other developers with a way to use your model. Now let's look at the API Gateway service in more detail.

AWS API Gateway

The API Gateway is a double service that allows you to create, publish, monitor, and secure APIs. We can connect the API Gateway not only to business Lambda but also to AWS EC2 instances, **Elastic Clusters (ECS)**, or even to **Elastic Beanstalk (EBS)**. It has a pay-as-you-go system, which makes it very convenient as a starting service. Let's look at the specific features of the API Gateway.

Features

The following are some of the features of the API Gateway:

- **Easy to scale**: The API service takes care of scaling, which means we do not have to worry as to whether this is a good way to handle peak loads, and whether it will over-provision resources.
- **Traffic management**: The API Gateway has a way to control the traffic. The main use case in traffic management is throttling when we want to have a more uniform load on the backend. This is not an issue with AWS Lambda, as it can scale almost indefinitely.

- **Authorization**: This allows you to control user access to the API. This means that we can either keep the API private or commercialize it. This feature is essential for your application.
- **Monitoring**: This feature enables us to get usage statistics at the user level. This is important if we want to limit users based on their usage, and if we need to troubleshoot our API.
- **Caching**: This allows you to reduce the amount of requests, which go to the backend by caching some of the responses. If your application has to deal with the load of repetitive requests, then the switch would significantly reduce the amount of usage at the backend.
- **Version control**: This allows you to manage multiple versions of the API, which is very important for the production of the application.

Now, let's look at the pricing of the API.

Pricing

One of the main advantages of the API Gateway is its pay-as-you-go feature. The pricing for the service amounts to 3.5 dollars per million requests and around 0.09 dollars per 1 GB of data transfer charges. Other optional charges may apply to the services that are chosen. Therefore, we need to make sure that it helps to reduce the cost of the backend. The cost we saw for the API Gateway can be extremely affordable for our project. For beginners, the AWS API Gateway is part of the free tier, and you can get 1 million requests per month for free. Kindly note that the free tier is only for new users.

Creating the API Gateway

Now that we are aware of the costing and features of the API Gateway, we will create the API Gateway using the AWS console. But before we start, we will need to create and locate AWS Lambda (created in Chapter 4, *Working with TensorFlow on AWS Lambda*), and then we will learn how to create a connection between the AWS API Gateway and AWS Lambda.

Creating an AWS Lambda instance

We will create the AWS Lambda instance and connect to a Gateway using the AWS console. Let's start with creating the AWS Lambda instance and choose the administrative role that we created in the previous chapter, as shown in the following screenshot:

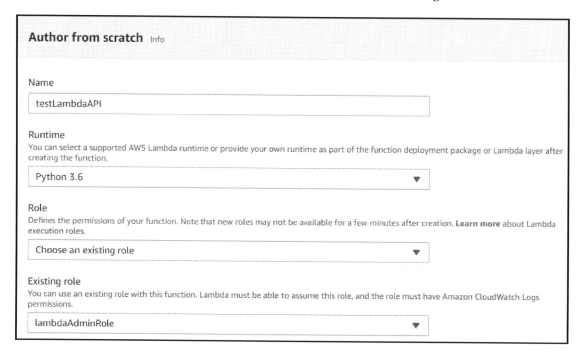

Let's test the function and check that it has been created using the **Test** option in the top-right side of the screen, as shown in the following screenshot:

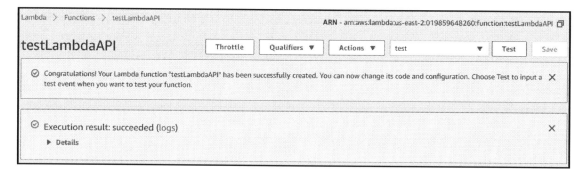

Now, let's add the API Gateway trigger by clicking on the **API Gateway** option on the left side under **Add triggers**. Now under the **Configure triggers** tab, select **Create a new API** and select an **Open** API endpoint. Now, under **Additional setting,** just check the API name and click on **Add** to create the API and save it. This will give you the page shown in the following screenshot, which has a link to the API to test on your browser:

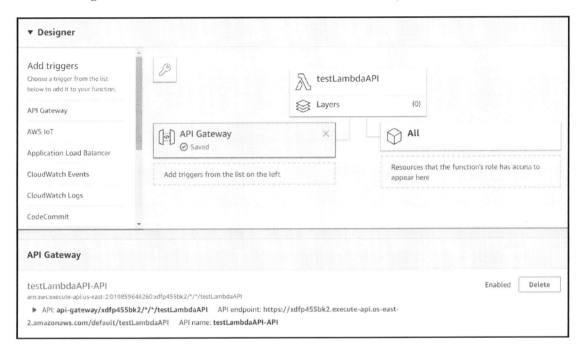

As you can see, it produced a result that is similar to the demo code, as seen in the following screenshot:

```
"Hello from Lambda!"
```

Now we are ready with the AWS Lambda and the API Gateway, we will be creating the connection using the serverless framework.

Creating the API Gateway using the serverless framework

Before creating the API, let us look at our project files: the main Python file (`index.py`) and the serverless configuration file (`serverless.yml`). Let's look at the Python file as shown in the following code:

```
import json
def handler(event, context):
print('Log event', event)
return{
'status code': 200;
'body': json.dump('Hello world API!')
}
```

From the preceding code block, you can see that this file will be returning a JSON response instead of the string to the API request. For this, we need to change `status code` to `200` and change `body` to `transform` in the JSON format.

In the server configuration file, we will be adding a `events` and adding an API endpoint name:

```
functions:
  main:
    handler: index.handler
    events:
      - http: GET hello
```

Deploying the serverless framework

Now let's deploy the service by using the following command:

```
serverless deploy
```

On successful completion of the deployment, it will return the URL for the API Gateway. Now test the URL we got on the command line using the `curl` command and URL:

```
endpoints:
  GET - https://be7dtg0vei.execute-api.us-east-1.amazonaws.com/dev/hello
functions:
  main: HelloWorldAPI-dev-main
layers:
  None

C:\Users\test\Desktop\V12024_Codes\B13880Code\lesson5.3>curl https://be7dtg0vei.execute-api.us-east-1.amazonaws.com/dev/hello
"Hello world API!"
```

We can also run the URL in the browser and test the deployment to find the desired output.

Creating a first API project

Now let us start by creating the example of the deep learning API project. Before we start the project, let's look at our files: the main Python file and the service configuration file, along with some libraries files and the inception model.

In this project, we will be adding one `events` section and the endpoint name. In the Python file, we will be returning a JSON response to a request. Also, we will make Lambda accept the link to the image in the request and then apply it to a module. The we will be deploying the server and testing the files in the command line and browser, as we checked out in the previous section.

The present configuration file is a combination of changes from the previous section and is very much similar. An additional part where are will be making a change is in the Python file, where we have added reading URL parameters. As you can see, if no URL is present, we use our image taken earlier. But, if we have the URL path, we can download the image from the URL.

Now let's deploy the service using the `serverless deploy` command, which will provide you with the URL of the API Gateway. Let's test this URL using the `curl` command and from the browser and you will find the same response that we had in the previous section:

```
["giant panda, panda, panda bear, coon bear, Ailuropoda melanoleuca (score = 0.89342)", "ice
bear, polar bear, Ursus Maritimus, Thalarctos maritimus (score = 0.00277)", "lesser panda, red
panda, panda, bear cat, cat bear, Ailurus fulgens (score = 0.00215)", "American black bear,
black bear, Ursus americanus, Euarctos americanus (score = 0.00143)", "brown bear, bruin,
Ursus arctos (score = 0.00122)"]
```

We can also test the deployment by downloading the image. To test this, we only have to add the URL of the image as a parameter to the API Gateway URL.

Summary

In this chapter, we learned about the API Gateway services and the RESTful API. We saw how the AWS Gateway is cost effective for our application. Then we looked at how to create the AWS API Gateway and AWS Lambda using the AWS console. We also created a connection between AWS Lambda and the AWS API Gateway using the serverless framework. Finally, we created the deep learning API project using the API Gateway.

In the next chapter, we will be creating crossing pipelines by connected and obvious Lambda little bills is curious where we will learn how to make a deep learning pipeline.

6
Creating a Deep Learning Pipeline

In the last chapter, we studied the creation of the API gateway service using the AWS Console, as well as the serverless framework. In this chapter, we will learn about creating SQS connections using the AWS console, as well as the serverless framework.

In this chapter we will cover the following topics:

- Message queue
- Introducing AWS simple query service
- Creating AWS SQS using AWS console and serverless framework
- Sample projects—deep learning pipeline

Technical Requirements

The technical requirements in this chapter are as follows:

- AWS subscription
- Python 3.6
- AWS CLI
- Serverless framework
- You can find all the codes at `https://github.com/PacktPublishing/Hands-On-Serverless-Deep-Learning-with-TensorFlow-and-AWS-Lambda`

Message queue

The message queue is an important additional method of interaction within different services. While the RESTful API has a timeout limit, the message queue doesn't have this kind of drawback. Therefore, it helps to handle long-running processes or delayed messages. Also, it allows a more uniform load on the backend. It does not have a critical feature for working with AWS Lambda, since Lambda can easily scale, but it can be very useful when dealing with clusters. Finally, the message queue allows retry logic, meaning that failed tasks can be sent back multiple times. Now let's look more into AWS SQS.

Introduction to AWS SQS

Basically, this is an AWS service that allows the sending, receipt, and storage of messages. It can be connected to any processing backend. It has a pay-as-you-go system, which makes it very convenient as a starting point.

AWS API gateway features

The different features of AWS API are as follows:

- It is extremely scalable, and you don't have to manage any other scaling in the queue.
- The service handles access from readers to the queue, so it's something that you don't have to implement.
- SQS has a customizable retry mechanism that increases the probability of avoiding errors, which improves the overall speed.
- SQS provides very simple APIs, which you can use in almost any programming language.
- Finally, it provides encryption, which could be useful for improving the security of your service.

AWS SQS pricing

One of the main advantages of SQS is the pay-per-user-go system, which is very simple. Pricing is 50 cents per 1 million requests and the first one million requests are free every month. This makes it perfect for early projects.

Creating an AWS SQS connection using an AWS Console

In this section, we will initially create an AWS Lambda, and then create the simple query service, before connecting SQS to AWS Lambda.

Creating an AWS Lambda instance

The following are the steps for creating the AWS Lambda instance:

1. First, add the name under **Name**, choose **Runtime** as **Python 3.6**, set **Role** as **Choose an existing role**, then from **Existing role** choose `lambda1`, and click on **Create function**, as shown here:

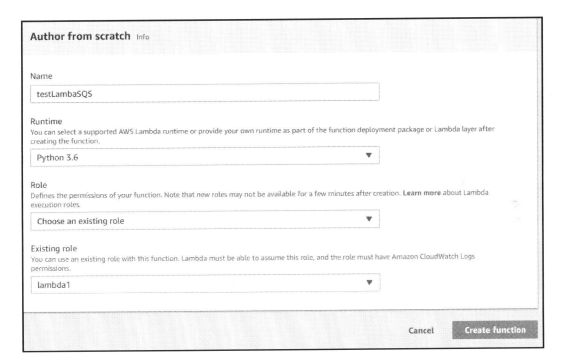

2. The Lambda function is created as shown in the following screenshot:

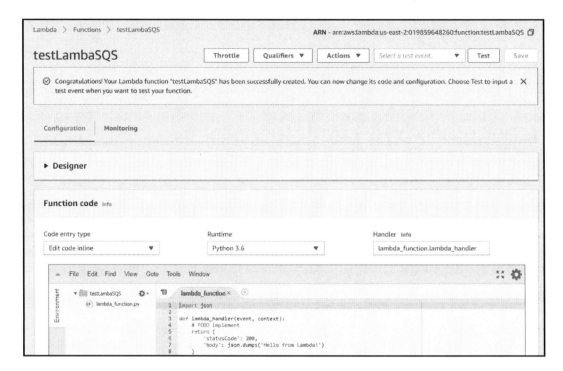

3. Next, switch to SQS and create a SQS queue by selecting **Create New Queue**:

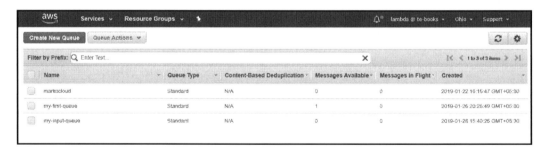

4. After creating a queue named **testLambda**, we get the SQS ARN as highlighted in the following screenshot:

5. From the **Designer** tab on the left, choose **SQS** as the trigger:

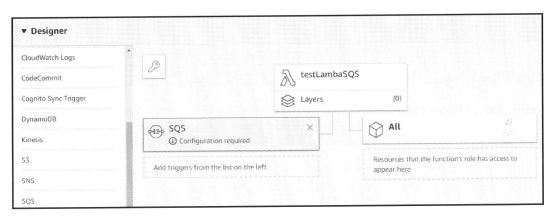

6. We will send some messages to the queue by selecting **Send a Message** from the **Queue Actions** drop-down list:

7. As you can see, we have only one message available, meaning they all were consumed by Lambda as shown in the following screenshot:

8. By clicking **Monitoring**, we get a detailed overview as shown:

9. We also get to see the log details by clicking on **View logs in CloudWatch** as shown in the preceding screeenshot. Each start and end means invocation for each message.

The next section concerns the creation of an AWS SQS connection to AWS Lambda using the serverless framework.

Creating an AWS SQS connection using the serverless framework

To create the SQS connection, we have the main Python file and the serverless configuration file. The configuration file will be a little complex. We will need to define SQS in the resources section, edit as event source for Lambda, and then enable Lambda to read from SQS.

The Python file

The main difference for the Python file will be that, instead of returning a string, we will write to another SQS query, as shown:

```
                                            Python File

def handler(event,context):

    print('Log event',event)

    writeToSQS(event)

    return 'Hello world'
```

Code

Before starting with the code, we will first need to deploy the serverless framework, and then we need to check that it runs using the command-line interface. We will run the code using the `index.py` file and the `serverless.yml` configuration file.

serverless.yml

In the `serverless.yml` file, we can see all the sections that we discussed in the previous chapters, especially the part where we define the role for accessing the query from where we will read messages, and to which our Lambda will write. The following code shows the explanation:

```
Effect: "Allow"
Action:
    "sqs:ReceiveMessage"
    "sqs:DeleteMessage"
    "sqs:GetQueueAttributes"
Resource:
    arn:aws:sqs:#{AWS::Region}:#{AWS::AccountId}:ReadSQS
```

We also have to define that one of the queries will act as an event source, as shown:

```
events:
    sqs:
      arn:
        Fn::GetAtt:
          ReadSQS
          Arn
```

Finally, we define the queries, which we can perform in the resource section as shown in the code:

```
resources:
  Resources:
    WriteSQS:
      Type: AWS::SQS::Queue
      Properties:
        QueueName: "WriteSQS"
    ReadSQS:
      Type: AWS::SQS::Queue
      Properties:
        QueueName: "ReadSQS"
```

Also, we will need to use the plugin `serverless-pseudo-parameters`, which we will install:

```
plugins:
  - serverless-pseudo-parameters
```

We will need to remove the package with the preceding plugin from the `deployment` package as shown:

```
package:
  exclude:
    - node_modules/**
```

Next is to use this plugin to access the ID of the region that we use and our account ID as shown:

```
Resource:
  - arn:aws:sqs:#{AWS::Region}:#{AWS::AccountId}:ReadSQS
Effect: "Allow"
Action:
  - "sqs:SendMessage"
  - "sqs:GetQueueUrl"
Resource:
  - arn:aws:sqs:#{AWS::Region}:#{AWS::AccountId}:WriteSQS
```

You can access the account ID and the ID of a region without this plugin and just manually find it as well.

index.py

The `index.py` file is very simple. We just read incoming messages and then write them as SQS. The following shows the code for `index.py`:

```
import boto3

def handler(event,context):
    for message in event['Records']:
        client = boto3.client('sqs')
        sqsAddress = client.get_queue_url(QueueName='WriteSQS')
        response = client.send_message(QueueUrl=sqsAddress['QueueUrl'],
                                       MessageBody=message['body'])
    return
```

We will see the preceding `index.py` and `serverless.yml` files in the command line:

First of all, we need to install plugin, `serverless-pseudo-parameters`:

```
npm install serverless-pseudo-parameters
```

The output is as follows:

```
C:\Users\test>npm install serverless-pseudo-parameters
npm WARN saveError ENOENT: no such file or directory, open 'C:\Users\test\package.json'
npm WARN enoent ENOENT: no such file or directory, open 'C:\Users\test\package.json'
npm WARN test No description
npm WARN test No repository field.
npm WARN test No README data
npm WARN test No license field.

+ serverless-pseudo-parameters@2.4.0
added 1 package and audited 2 packages in 1.352s
found 0 vulnerabilities
```

Next, we will deploy Lambda using the following command:

```
serverless deploy
```

As you can see, the plugin replaced the region with the actual base region and account as shown in the following screenshot:

```
Serverless: Stack update finished...
Service Information
service: HelloWorldSQS
stage: dev
region: us-east-1
stack: HelloWorldSQS-dev
api keys:
  None
endpoints:
  None
functions:
  main: HelloWorldSQS-dev-main
layers:
  None
```

To send a message through the queue, first we need to find the queue URL using the following command:

```
aws sqs get-queue-url --queue-name ReadSQS
```

With the queue URL, we can send messages. We see the command executed successfully here:

```
{
    "QueueUrl": "https://queue.amazonaws.com/339543757547/ReadSQS"
}
Rustems-MacBook-Pro:lesson6.3 ryfeus$ aws sqs send-message --queue-u
rl https://sqs.us-east-1.amazonaws.com/339543757547/ReadSQS --messag
e-body "Hello world1"
{
    "MD5OfMessageBody": "afe41d633b5d19c1a5b779a55be9d7b0",
    "MessageId": "5f97e1ef-0801-493c-8854-4c076a35a0bf"
}
```

Now we can read the same message from the SQS queue. Basically, here we can check whether Lambda has received the message that we have sent, which is `Hello world1`, and send it to write SQL. We see that Lambda works successfully and we can see the resulting message, `Hello world1`, in the following screenshot:

```
}
Rustems-MacBook-Pro:lesson6.3 ryfeus$ aws sqs receive-message --queu
e-url https://sqs.us-east-1.amazonaws.com/339543757547/WriteSQS
{
    "Messages": [
        {
            "MessageId": "2fbae850-1232-4688-9a0d-f4edec62eb10",
            "ReceiptHandle": "AQEBUQPqDXjvwYX1bXTsQspDjwMQq4P8WcKpga
RCJB/NV71YN4YvGMSLNy9KU8BKuJSW18dUN+BgtEBeongT7lXpfNdzEXm3uEuL3AamAe
+QLZ4gFJqhHupGHACxIHkOE1WtKvkK8GPmkjZKLg2ZAqFMx/TRisOlf6jCSLiGA3ZB3V
QgKvvelGTNuAMnin93Pi/KT2iwzpDOx1u3vjFxgnLUvBMWGEvVp00rrsfLSF2rqyUkdi
DDtb3M6gw6ymolO2mRcp6wiTrI7jCq2dByzp83wwcMyrVNEzR1nyOt1sG2U1hH16FKky
Tv4VEW1kUXUqfOmPiG0BOJ+JW5d889tW9tRv0/Oorx4V2LHsrkLn+6eGO5ec1iRnxxdK
4CrSNgpRXp",
            "MD5OfBody": "afe41d633b5d19c1a5b779a55be9d7b0",
            "Body": "Hello world1"
        }
    ]
```

Example project – deep learning pipeline

In the project files, we have the main Python file, the serverless configuration file, libraries files, and an inception module. The configuration file will be the same as the one we used in the previous chapter. We will look at the Python file. The main difference for our Python file will be that, instead of returning the string, we will send a message to another SQS query. Also, we will make Lambda accept the link to the image in the message, and then apply module to structure it. The deployment will be similar to the one in the previous section.

We will skip the deployment of the model, since we have covered it before.

Code

First, we will need to deploy the serverless framework, and then we can check that it runs using the command-line interface. We have the `index.py` file and the `serverless.yml` configuration file. We also have libraries for TensorFlow and pre-installed plugins for the serverless framework.

Configuration file - serverless.yml

We can see that the current configuration file is taken from the preceding sections.

We have a bucket where we keep our model, as shown in the following code snippet:

```
Effect: "Allow"
Action:
  - "s3:ListBucket"
Resource:
  - arn:aws:s3:::serverlessdeeplearning
Effect: "Allow"
Action:
  - "s3:GetObject"
Resource:
  - arn:aws:s3:::serverlessdeeplearning/*
```

There is an event source for Lambda and resources, as shown in the following code snippet:

```
- sqs:
    arn:
      Fn::GetAtt:
        - DLReadSQS
        - Arn
```

index.py

In the `index.py` file, the script looks the same way as it did in the previous section. An additional part has been added, which is reading the URL from the message and writing the result to another queue. The following is the code snippet for `index.py`:

```
import boto3
import numpy as np
import tensorflow as tf
import os.path
import re
from urllib.request import urlretrieve
```

```
import json
SESSION = None
strBucket = 'serverlessdeeplearning'
def handler(event, context):
    global strBucket
    global SESSION
    if not os.path.exists('/tmp/imagenet/'):
        os.makedirs('/tmp/imagenet/')
        ...
```

The following screenshot shows the part where we retrieve the image and run our model on it, and hence, we write the result of the model to another queue, as shown:

```
if ('Records' in event):
    for message in event['Records']:
        urlretrieve(message['body'].strip('\''), strFile)
        vecResult = run_inference_on_image(strFile)
        client = boto3.client('sqs')
        sqsAddress = client.get_queue_url(QueueName='DLWriteSQS')
        response = client.send_message(QueueUrl=sqsAddress['QueueUrl'],
                                MessageBody=vecResult[0])
else:
        downloadFromS3(strBucket,'imagenet/inputimage.png',strFile)
        strResult = run_inference_on_image(strFile)
```

Now let's deploy the service as shown:

```
Serverless: Stack update finished...
Service Information
service: DeepLearningPipeline
stage: dev
region: us-east-1
stack: DeepLearningPipeline-dev
api keys:
  None
endpoints:
  None
functions:
  main: DeepLearningPipeline-dev-main
layers:
  None
```

We will send the message with a URL to the first queue. This can be done with the command-line interface:

```
Rustems-MacBook-Pro:lesson6.4 ryfeus$ aws sqs send-message --queue-u
rl https://sqs.us-east-1.amazonaws.com/339543757547/DLReadSQS --mess
age-body "'https://images.unsplash.com/photo-1529429617124-95b109e86
bb8?ixlib=rb-0.3.5&ixid=eyJhcHBfaWQiOjEyMDd9&s=6a14f6903383d2e97411b
e5015dbc68f&auto=format&fit=crop&w=1000&q=60'"
{
    "MD5OfMessageBody": "172eaf99e91466c071b14d95b906df41",
    "MessageId": "a6954e6f-90a7-4c2b-a301-51ba6fc4240b"
}
Rustems-MacBook-Pro:lesson6.4 ryfeus$ serverless deploy
```

We can read the sent message from another queue as shown here:

```
Rustems-MacBook-Pro:lesson6.4 ryfeus$ aws sqs receive-message --queu
e-url https://sqs.us-east-1.amazonaws.com/339543757547/DLWriteSQS
{
    "Messages": [
        {
            "MessageId": "7106c321-53d6-4d6e-a799-49d8636100d4",
            "ReceiptHandle": "AQEB/nfbyutQk7tb+b5YtP4UMNEyjbs15/ENp6
Fso1N1SCTrbKolgHbLPHuMuMKzHSVTGpqxQz1O8VGXsT5zWqVAWtysXfpJzrp+/7V0cR
5CnfN1Koce2gipArREz+OJ1/iGzHJOJvSO/OdaR0Uv1mk1QG4WLNJaqpXg7Ad5MSYQy5
GPELPSiIov1rYbBEftR/6son7toR9V7j650bihcSzXOQq7n+4jxaGzKdz1nFg+MTPQzv
fQMdedPp54lyOGTtaNFnzjPVCL4OElbWoSwivun8Hr7xkSP4k4eHEzY7CeNQcsLLZ/Qv
Ziy1+FtjgajA9QBZl1j7Xpvb95s24EvWHzzeFL8Vv9sA0JzworuRVWQIBHbiI8EMyYm+
kYBe8ssZgn",
            "MD5OfBody": "ff42fb7631d8f81da219c6085f0471ea",
            "Body": "Samoyed, Samoyede (score = 0.82913)"
        }
    ]
```

Summary

In this chapter, we were introduced to AWS SQS, which included the features as well as a look at its pricing. We also created AWS SQS connection using both the AWS console and the serverless framework.

We learned about the deployment of the `serverless.yml` configuration file and the `index.py` file. This chapter concluded with an example project, which was a deep learning pipeline.

In the next chapter, we will learn about creating crossing workflow by connecting an AWS Lambda instance and AWS functions where we will learn how to make deep learning workflow.

7
Creating a Deep Learning Workflow

In this chapter, you will learn about the AWS Step Functions service and also create AWS step functions by connecting to AWS Lambda using the AWS Console. You will also learn to create an AWS step function connection using the serverless framework and finally you will look into an example project for a deep learning workflow.

We will cover the following topics:

- Introduction to the AWS Step Functions service
- Creating an AWS Step Functions connection to AWS Lambda using the AWS Console
- Creating an AWS Step Functions connection using the serverless framework
- Deep learning workflow

Technical requirements

The technical requirements for this chapter are as follows:

- AWS subscription
- Python 3.6
- AWS CLI
- Serverless framework
- You can find all the code at `https://github.com/PacktPublishing/Hands-On-Serverless-Deep-Learning-with-TensorFlow-and-AWS-Lambda`

Introduction to the AWS Step Functions service

In this section, we will cover the AWS Step Functions service, including its features and also the pricing for using this service.

Processing workflow

The processing workflow is an additional method for interaction between the different services. If you want to build a multi-step process in deep learning, it could mean loading the data, then pre-processing data and running the model on it. While you can put queries between each of these backend nodes, it would be very hard to monitor the processing for a single task. This is where the workflow can be extremely convenient. Basically, the workflow service takes care of the invocation of each node when needed and handles the intermediate state of the processing job. It allows you to have a high-level view of what is happening with each task, and track task failures and timeouts. Finally, it allows you to have very flexible component usage as part of the workflow.

AWS Step Functions

AWS Step Function is an AWS service that allows you to manage the workflow as a state machine. It can be connected to any processing backend and has a native integration with AWS Lambda. It has a pay-as-you-go system, which makes it very convenient.

AWS step function features

We will now look at the specific features of step functions:

- Step functions are extremely scalable and you don't have to manage neither the scanning nor the workflow.
- Step functions have a great visual UI, which enables easy monitoring of the processing jobs.
- State management allows you to add complex logic, such as choosing the next node based on the results of previous nodes, and it also allows for running several nodes in parallel.

- Some functions have convenient logic for retrying tasks, which enables you to ensure processing.
- Built-in error handling allows you to handle cases. For example, when you encounter some exception and you need a way to add logic for error handling, such as marking a task as failed in the database.
- Scheduling allows you to run delayed processing tasks, which is very convenient for when you have to wait for another process to complete.

AWS Step Functions pricing

One of the main advantages of step functions is the pay-as-you go system. It is very simple 25 cents per 10,000 requests, of which the first 4,000 requests are free per month. This makes it perfect for early projects.

Step functions versus SQS

If we dive deep into how the step functions are different from SQS in terms of features and possible use cases, we can say that SQS is most suitable for short, simple, low-priority tasks that can come in very large volumes (millions of tasks per day). Step functions, on the other hand, are most suitable for cases where we have complex multi-step processes, which can take a lot of time and where we would like to guarantee delivery of every task (thousands of tasks per day). In the next section, you will learn how to create an AWS Step Functions connection to AWS Lamda using the AWS Console.

Creating an AWS Step Functions connection to AWS Lambda using the AWS Console

In this section, we will create setp functions using the AWS Console. To create a step function, there are two main steps:

1. Creating the AWS Lambda instance
2. Creating the step function that will use the Lambda instance

Creating the AWS Lambda instance

Now we will create an AWS Lambda instance using the AWS Console:

1. Navigate to Lambda to create the Lambda instance.
2. Now enter the **Name** as `testLambdaStepFunction`, **Runtime** as **Python 3.6**, **Role** as **Choose an existing role,** and the existing role as `lamdaAdminRole`. Then click on **Create function,** which is at the bottom-right part of the screen:

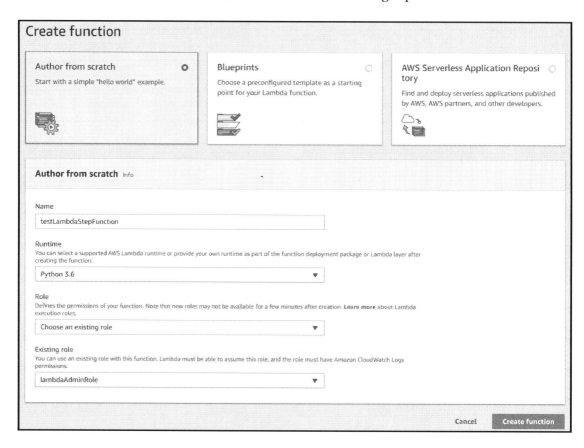

3. The Lambda instance has been successfully created:

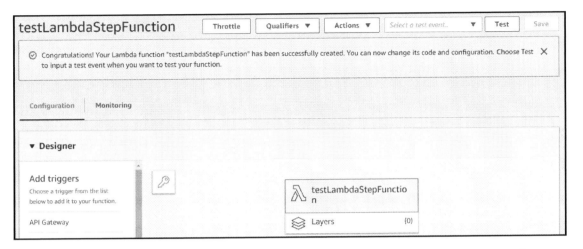

Creating the step function

To create the step function, we need to perform the following steps:

1. Go to the Step Functions service and click on **Create state machine**:

2. In the **Define state machine** tab, enter the name as `testLambda`:

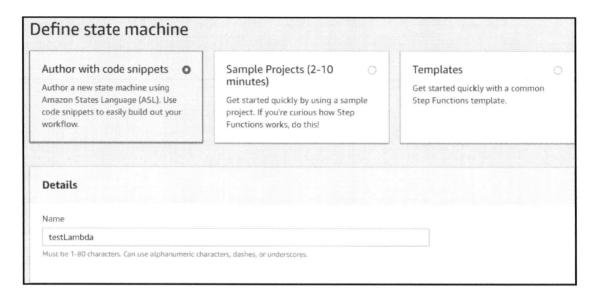

3. Now we need to define `Type` as `Task` and the `Resource`. For the resource, you will need to use the ARN address of your Lambda, which you will find in the top-right corner of the tab. You can copy and paste this in the state machine definition section, as shown in the following screenshot:

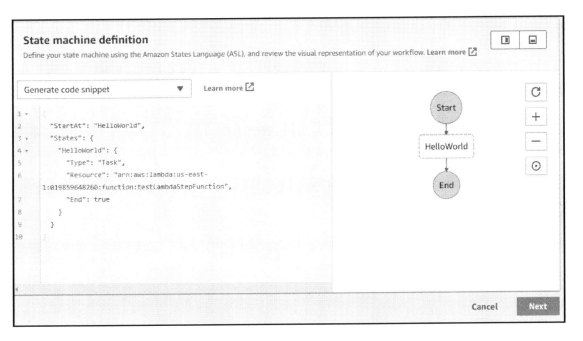

4. We will now create an IAM role, which is done automatically. Enter the name as `StepFunctionTestRole` and click on **Create function.** This will take up a minute before your state machine has permissions to execute properly:

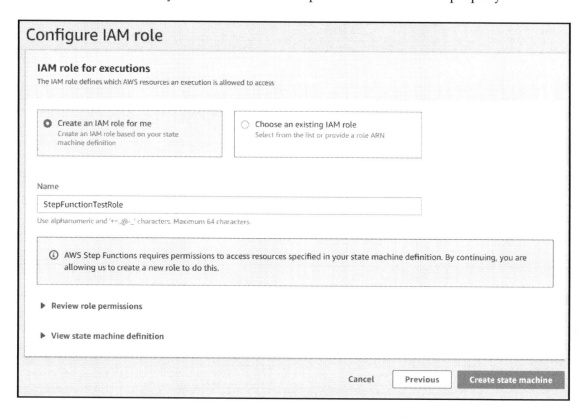

5. Now, once we have created the step function, we can test and send a simple message. To do this, click on **Start execution**:

6. We can see the graph of execution here:

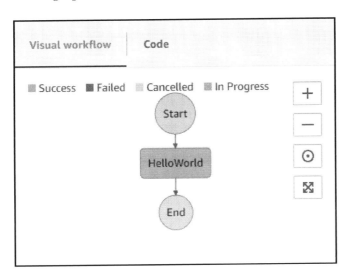

7. For each execution, you can see the input and output of the whole step function:

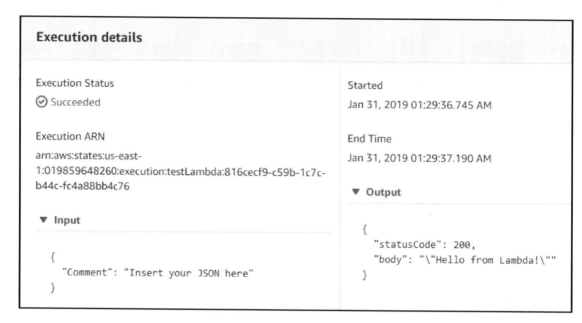

Execution details

Execution Status

⊘ Succeeded

Execution ARN

arn:aws:states:us-east-
1:019859648260:execution:testLambda:816cecf9-c59b-1c7c-
b44c-fc4a88bb4c76

▼ **Input**

```
{
  "Comment": "Insert your JSON here"
}
```

Started

Jan 31, 2019 01:29:36.745 AM

End Time

Jan 31, 2019 01:29:37.190 AM

▼ **Output**

```
{
  "statusCode": 200,
  "body": "\"Hello from Lambda!\""
}
```

8. We can see the input and output of each node (this can be seen in the **Step details** tab). If there is an error, we will be able to see it in the **Exception** tab. Also, if you scroll down, you can also see the timeline of execution:

Step details (HelloWorld)

Status

⊘ Succeeded

Resource

arn:aws:lambda:us-east-
1:019859648260:function:testLambdaStepFunction |
CloudWatch logs

▼ Input

```
{
  "Comment": "Insert your JSON here"
}
```

▼ Output

```
{
  "statusCode": 200,
  "body": "\"Hello from Lambda!\""
}
```

▼ Exception

9. We can also check logs by using the link present in the **Resource** tab under the **Step details** tab by clicking on it. This will lead you to the following page:

Therefore, we can see that step function is a very convenient service for managing Lambda execution.

Creating AWS step functions for an AWS Lambda instance using the serverless framework

In this section, we'll create step functions using the serverless framework. First, let's take a look at our project files: one Python file and the serverless configuration file. In the configuration file, we will be adding a few plugins and describing step functions, which is a complex thing.

So, let's explore the step functions in the serverless configuration file by beginning with the live code:

1. Deploy the serverless framework.
2. Using the CLI, check the deployment status of the serverless framework.
3. Now, check the step function result using the AWS Console.

Step functions

Let's check the list of files that we have by executing the `ls` command. As you can see, we have the `index.py` file and the `serverless.yml` configuration file service document. We also have installed plugins for the serverless framework.

Let's take a look at the configuration file and its two main parts here:

1. First, we will be adding several functions, which will be used in different states of the step function:

```
function:
    branch:
        handler: index.handlerBranch
    map:
        handler: index.handlerMap
    reduce:
        handler: index.handlerReduce
```

2. Next, we will add some plugins, which are required to work with step functions:

```
plugins:     - serverless-step-functions
         - serverless-pseudo-parameters
```

3. Now let's take a look at the index.py file, where you can see all the parts discussed so far:

```
def handlerMap(event,context):
    return event

def handlerReduce(event,context):
    return event

def handlerBranch(event,context):
    return 'Hello world'
```

Serverless deployment

Now, let's deploy our service by executing the following command:

```
serverless deploy
```

The preceding command deploys your service, as shown in the following screenshot:

```
AWS Pseudo Parameter: Resources::HelloWorldStepFunction::Properties:
:DefinitionString Replaced AWS::Region with ${AWS::Region}
AWS Pseudo Parameter: Resources::HelloWorldStepFunction::Properties:
:DefinitionString Replaced AWS::AccountId with ${AWS::AccountId}
AWS Pseudo Parameter: Resources::HelloWorldStepFunction::Properties:
:DefinitionString Replaced AWS::Region with ${AWS::Region}
AWS Pseudo Parameter: Resources::HelloWorldStepFunction::Properties:
:DefinitionString Replaced AWS::AccountId with ${AWS::AccountId}
AWS Pseudo Parameter: Resources::HelloWorldStepFunction::Properties:
:DefinitionString Replaced AWS::Region with ${AWS::Region}
AWS Pseudo Parameter: Resources::HelloWorldStepFunction::Properties:
:DefinitionString Replaced AWS::AccountId with ${AWS::AccountId}
AWS Pseudo Parameter: Resources::HelloWorldStepFunction::Properties:
:DefinitionString Replaced AWS::Region with ${AWS::Region}
AWS Pseudo Parameter: Resources::HelloWorldStepFunction::Properties:
:DefinitionString Replaced AWS::AccountId with ${AWS::AccountId}
```

As part of the deployment, it will give us the URL of the API Gateway, as shown in the following screenshot:

```
endpoints:
  GET - https://dns1519i1j.execute-api.us-east-1.amazonaws.com/dev/s
tartFunction
```

Now let's test the URL in the command line:

```
curl
https://dns1519i1j.execute-api.us-east-1.amazonaws.com/dev/startFunction
```

You can check with the results in your browser. In the following screenshot, you can see our step function:

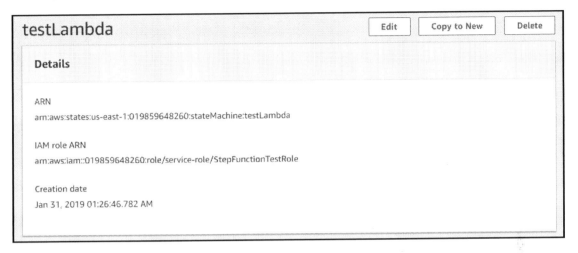

In the following screenshot, we can see that the latest execution went successfully:

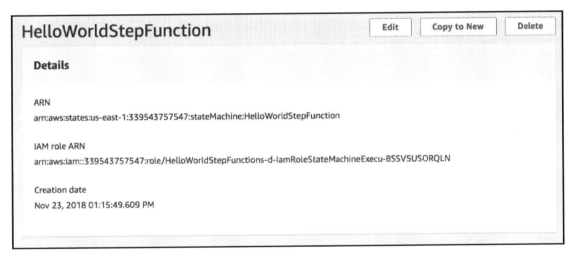

You can check the input and output of each node. If there are any errors, you can check them in the **Exception** section.

Both branches returned hello world and the step node combines the result and returns it as the result of the step function:

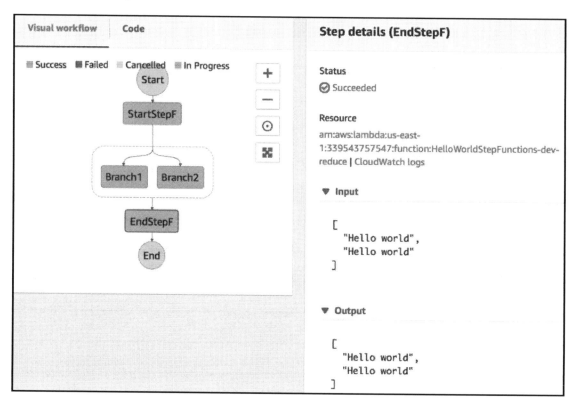

Here, let's check with the timeline of the execution. You can also see that the branches have started almost at the same time.

In the next section, we will look at an example of the deep learning workflow project.

Example project – deep learning workflow

First, let's take a look at our following project files. We have the main Python file, the service integration file, and a few libraries and inception models. In the configuration file, we will be adding a few plugins and describing step functions, which is a complex thing.

The main difference with our Python file will be that we will have three functions . One will map a list of URL links into separate things. Another will run a model on the link. The final one will combine the results. The structure of the deployment will be similar to the one in the previous section. We will skip the deployment of the model to S3, since we covered it in the previous chapter.

Creating the model

Here, we will need to deploy the serverless framework and then we can check the trance using the CLI:

1. Let's look at the configuration file. You can see all the main parts and roles that we need to define to access the model:

```
provider:
  name: aws
  region: us-east-1
  runtime: python3.6
  memorySize: 1536
  timeout: 30
  iamRoleStatements:
    - Effect: "Allow"
      Action:
        - "s3:ListBucket"
      Resource:
        - arn:aws:s3:::serverlessdeeplearning
    - Effect: "Allow"
      Action:
        - "s3:GetObject"
      Resource:
        - arn:aws:s3:::serverlessdeeplearning/*
```

2. Here are the functions, which we will use in different states of the step function:

```
functions:
  main:
    handler: index.handler
  map:
    handler: index.map
  reduce:
    handler: index.reduce
```

3. `map` will enable the mapping of the incoming event into different Lambdas, range will enable the processing of each link separately in parallel, and `reduce` will help in combining them in one response. We have the state machine definition, which is very similar to that previously discussed:

```
stepFunctions:
  stateMachines:
    DeepLearningWorkflow:
      events:
        - http:
            path: gofunction
            method: POST
      name: DeepLearningWorkflow
      definition:
        StartAt: StartStepF
        States:
          StartStepF:
            Type: Task
            Resource:
arn:aws:lambda:#{AWS::Region}:#{AWS::AccountId}:function:${self:ser
vice}-${opt:stage}-map
            Next: Parallel
          Parallel:
            Type: Parallel
            Next: EndStepF
            Branches:
              - StartAt: Branch1
                States:
                  Branch1:
                    Type: Task
                    Resource:
arn:aws:lambda:#{AWS::Region}:#{AWS::AccountId}:function:${self:ser
vice}-${opt:stage}-main
                    InputPath: '$.branch1.url'
                    ResultPath: '$.res'
                    End: True
              - StartAt: Branch2
                States:
                  Branch2:
                    Type: Task
                    Resource:
arn:aws:lambda:#{AWS::Region}:#{AWS::AccountId}:function:${self:ser
vice}-${opt:stage}-main
                    InputPath: '$.branch2.url'
                    ResultPath: '$.res'
                    End: True
              - StartAt: Branch3
```

```
States:
    Branch3:
        Type: Task
        Resource:
arn:aws:lambda:#{AWS::Region}:#{AWS::AccountId}:function:${self:ser
vice}-${opt:stage}-main
            InputPath: '$.branch3.url'
            ResultPath: '$.res'
            End: True
    EndStepF:
        Type: Task
        Resource:
arn:aws:lambda:#{AWS::Region}:#{AWS::AccountId}:function:${self:ser
vice}-${opt:stage}-reduce
        End: true
```

4. Here, we have plugins, which are required to work the functions:

```
plugins:
    - serverless-step-functions
    - serverless-pseudo-parameters
```

5. The main difference in our index file from the previous section is that we added the MapReduce logic. This will enable the processing of each URL separately:

```
def map(event, context):
    dictMap = {}
    dictMap['branch1'] = {'url':event[0]}
    dictMap['branch2'] = {'url':event[1]}
    dictMap['branch3'] = {'url':event[2]}
    return dictMap

def reduce(event, context):
    vecRes = []
    for res in event:
        vecRes.append(res['res'])
    return vecRes
```

For this case, we'll have three URLs,for the dog, panda, and red panda images taken from the free images website.

6. Now we have our model ready, let's deploy the service using the following command:

```
serverless deploy
```

7. You will have the URL for the API to test.

8. Let's test this URL. We will need to use the `curl` command, which will be a little different from its usages previously.

9. First of all, we will use POST requests instead of GET requests, and we will provide a list of links as both of the request. As you can see, it returned successfully. This execution indicates that it successfully sent the command to the step function:

```
Rustems-MacBook-Pro:lesson7.4 ryfeus$ curl --header "Content-Type: a
pplication/json"    --request POST    --data '["https://images.unsplas
h.com/photo-1525382455947-f319bc05fb35?ixlib=rb-0.3.5&ixid=eyJhcHBfa
WQiOjEyMDd9&s=c69b7bad72e5863bf7c547c7bbe90b0a&auto=format&fit=crop&
w=1414&q=80","https://images.unsplash.com/photo-1463436755683-3f805a
9d1192?ixlib=rb-0.3.5&ixid=eyJhcHBfaWQiOjEyMDd9&s=4f9a76ae4a640e02f8
613da481c7c843&auto=format&fit=crop&w=1953&q=80","https://images.uns
plash.com/photo-1535930749574-1399327ce78f?ixlib=rb-0.3.5&ixid=eyJhc
HBfaWQiOjEyMDd9&s=1f8a140ac20927deb386d1c9187433d6&auto=format&fit=c
rop&w=976&q=80"]' https://2grw99308b.execute-api.us-east-1.amazonaws
.com/dev/gofunction
```

10. Now let's look at the graph in the browser. We can see that it has already finished the execution:

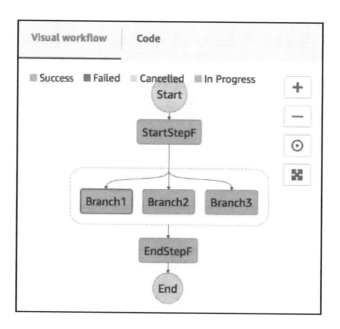

11. We can see that each branch received a separate URL, and we can see that the final note combined results from different branches as single, and that it successfully recognized the images:

```json
{
  "branch1": {
    "url":
"https://images.unsplash.com/photo-
1525382455947-f319bc05fb35?ixlib=rb-
0.3.5&ixid=eyJhcHBfaWQiOjEyMDd9&s=c69b7bad72
e5863bf7c547c7bbe90b0a&auto=format&fit=crop&
w=1414&q=80"
  },
  "branch2": {
    "url":
"https://images.unsplash.com/photo-
1463436755683-3f805a9d1192?ixlib=rb-
0.3.5&ixid=eyJhcHBfaWQiOjEyMDd9&s=4f9a76ae4a
640e02f8613da481c7c843&auto=format&fit=crop&
w=1953&q=80"
  },
  "branch3": {
    "url":
"https://images.unsplash.com/photo-
1535930749574-1399327ce78f?ixlib=rb-
0.3.5&ixid=eyJhcHBfaWQiOjEyMDd9&s=1f8a140ac2
0927deb386d1c9187433d6&auto=format&fit=crop&
w=976&q=80"
  }
}
```

Also, we can check the timeline of the execution and see that almost all the branches started at the same time.

This means that the parallelization really enabled us to process a list of links faster.

Summary

In this chapter, we studied the AWS Step Functions service, including its features and pricing. We also learned how to connect AWS Step Functions to AWS Lambda using the AWS Console. We also saw how to create a step function using the serverless framework and even created a deep learning workflow.

Other Books You May Enjoy

If you enjoyed this book, you may be interested in these other books by Packt:

TensorFlow Machine Learning Cookbook
Nick McClure

ISBN: 9781786462169

- Become familiar with the basics of the TensorFlow machine learning library
- Get to know Linear Regression techniques with TensorFlow
- Learn SVMs with hands-on recipes
- Implement neural networks and improve predictions
- Apply NLP and sentiment analysis to your data
- Master CNN and RNN through practical recipes
- Take TensorFlow into production

Machine Learning with AWS

Jeffrey Jackovich, Ruze Richards

ISBN: 9781789806199

- Get up and running with machine learning on the AWS platform
- Analyze unstructured text using AI and Amazon Comprehend
- Create a chatbot and interact with it using speech and text input
- Retrieve external data via your chatbot
- Develop a natural language interface
- Apply AI to images and videos with Amazon Rekognition

Leave a review - let other readers know what you think

Please share your thoughts on this book with others by leaving a review on the site that you bought it from. If you purchased the book from Amazon, please leave us an honest review on this book's Amazon page. This is vital so that other potential readers can see and use your unbiased opinion to make purchasing decisions, we can understand what our customers think about our products, and our authors can see your feedback on the title that they have worked with Packt to create. It will only take a few minutes of your time, but is valuable to other potential customers, our authors, and Packt. Thank you!

Index